Where Hearts are Shared
COOKBOOK

JANE HANSEN
GENERAL EDITOR

Regal

A Division of Gospel Light
Ventura, California, U.S.A.

PUBLISHED BY REGAL BOOKS
A DIVISION OF GOSPEL LIGHT
VENTURA, CALIFORNIA, U.S.A.
PRINTED IN THE U.S.A.

Regal Books is a ministry of Gospel Light, an evangelical Christian publisher dedicated to serving the local church. We believe God's vision for Gospel Light is to provide church leaders with biblical, user-friendly materials that will help them evangelize, disciple and minister to children, youth and families.

It is our prayer that this Regal book will help you discover biblical truth for your own life and help you meet the needs of others. May God richly bless you.

For a free catalog of resources from Regal Books/Gospel Light, please call your Christian supplier or contact us at 1-800-4-GOSPEL or www.regalbooks.com.

All Scripture quotations, unless otherwise indicated, are taken from the *New King James Version*.
Copyright © 1979, 1980, 1982 by Thomas Nelson, Inc. Used by permission. All rights reserved.
The other version used is: *KJV—King James Version*. Authorized King James Version.

Cover and Interior Design by Robert Williams
Edited by Deena Davis

Library of Congress Cataloging-in-Publication Data
Where hearts are shared / Jane Hansen, general editor.
p.c.
Includes index.
ISBN 0-8307-2893-7
1. Cookery.   2. Entertaining.   I. Hansen, Jane.
TX714.W485 2001
641.5—dc21   2001041672

1   2   3   4   5   6   7   8   9   10   11   12   13   14   15   /   09   08   07   06   05   04   03   02   01

Rights for publishing this book in other languages are contracted by Gospel Literature International (GLINT). GLINT also provides technical help for the adaptation, translation and publishing of Bible study resources and books in scores of languages worldwide. For further information, contact GLINT, P.O. Box 4060, Ontario, CA 91761-1003, U.S.A. You may also send e-mail to Glintint@aol.com, or visit their website at www.glint.org.

Contents

A Glimpse of Other Cultures

Preface

For most of us, the word "home" conjures up wonderful memories. I know it has always held a most important place in my life. The scent of baking bread coming from my grandmother's kitchen or the warm apple pie being served at my mother's Sunday table made home seem a wonderful gathering place, a place where hearts were shared around the table. Later, as a wife, mother and grandmother, one of my greatest joys has been to create that same warm, inviting atmosphere for other people. When I think of special occasions that have touched my life and heart in lasting ways, they have almost always taken place in a home, around a table, with family and friends.

In recent months, we have heard much about making our homes lighthouses—places that radiate the warmth, peace and light of Christ—for family, friends and neighbors. But at one time in American, women were often literally the keepers of lighthouses. They kept the lamps burning night after night—a difficult task with the oil lamps needing to be replenished at regular intervals all through the night. Yet these women were willing to endure the hardships of those long nights to save many a life.

One such woman, Catherine Moore, was keeper of the Black Rock Lighthouse in Connecticut from 1817 to 1879. She described her life's work:

> During windy nights it was almost impossible to keep [the lanterns] burning at all, so I had to stay there all night. On calm nights I slept at home, dressed, with my lighted lantern hanging on my headboard. I kept my face turned so I could see, shining on the wall, the light from the tower and know if anything had happened. If the light went out I got up to tend it.*

Her house was a distance from the tower, so Catherine had to walk across two planks under which, on stormy nights, were four feet of water. It was not easy to stay on the slippery, wet planks with the force of the wind and sea spray blinding her. But storms and gales were part of her life. In the 62 years she was at Black Rock, she saved many lives. Others, who washed up on shore half dead, she would revive and bring to her home where she fed and cared for

them and sent them on their way once again restored to health—all the while keeping the light on in the lighthouse each night!

When I think of women like Catherine, I am reminded of the virtuous woman of Proverbs 31:18 whose "lamp does not go out by night"—women who stay alert in dark, hard times, face into the "wind" and through prayer, the Word and serving others, bring the light of God to bear on seemingly impossible circumstances.

Jesus said, "I have come as a light into the world, that whoever believes in Me should not abide in darkness" (John 12:46). In Mathew 5:14 He declares that we are the bearers of that light, and in verse 16, He urges us to "let [our] light so shine before men [and women], that they may see your good works and glorify your Father in heaven." The light of our facing into the hard times and caring for others who are hurting or shipwrecked by life will lead them to the true light and glorify God.

My desire is that you will feel encouraged by this book to let your light shine! Too often we, the light-bearers of the home, struggle with lack of confidence when inviting guests into our homes. Yet we don't have to feel that way. I believe hospitality can be done simply yet beautifully!

In these pages you will discover not only delicious recipes and helpful entertaining tips from leaders all over the world, but you'll also find some easy-to-do decorating helps as well as inspirational thoughts. I know you will be inspired to allow the Lord to use you as one of His beacons of light right where He has placed you.

—Jane Hansen, President
Aglow International

*Mary Louise Clifford and J. Candace Clifford, *Women Who Kept the Lights: An Illustrated History of Female Lighthouse Keepers* (Alexandria, VA: Cypress Communications, 1995), n.p.

Acknowledgments

I would like to offer special thanks to my friend Carolyn Jones, who has worked tirelessly since the inception of this book. I appreciate her expertise as a former home economics teacher, as well as her tremendous organizational abilities. She took an unformed substance and gave it form.

I would also like to acknowledge Deena Davis, of Regal Books, who has helped "put it all together" and brought this book to the point of publishing. Thank you, Deena, for a great job!

A thank-you to Joan Bennett, who serves as my assistant and plays a significant but unseen role in so many ways.

And, of course, a word of gratitude to all the wonderful women who have shared their recipes, helpful hints and insights gained from their experiences in entertaining.

And a special thank-you to Deena Wilson for her delightful contributions. Deena, you have such a unique touch.

Hospitality Is Dear to God's Heart

[Be] a lover of hospitality.
TITUS 1:8, *KJV*

Hospitality is very dear to the heart of God. When we give ourselves to hospitality, we are creating a wonderful opportunity to serve the Lord and share His life in the most natural way in the world. Simply by showing ourselves friendly and gracious in the relaxed setting of our homes, we can tangibly and practically minister the life of Jesus to others.

In Romans 12, Paul provides a list of ways that we are to conduct ourselves as Christians and tells us that we are to be a people "given to hospitality" (v. 13). Hospitality is also one of the qualifications for those who are in leadership in the church (see 1 Tim. 3:2).

How should we be hospitable? Webster, in his unabridged dictionary, defines hospitable as "fond of entertaining guests in a friendly, generous manner. To be receptive and open."

In *Strong's Concordance* the hospitable person is described as "One who entertains strangers . . . is fond of guests . . . is given to or a lover of hospitality . . . is a friend or is friendly."

As people given to hospitality, our goal is to provide a relaxed, warm setting where the Holy Spirit can work in people's hearts. For this to happen, you, as the hostess, must be relaxed. Your guests will feel your internal state—either your nervousness or your ease.

Keep in mind that the success of the evening is not based on what you cook or how you serve it but on how welcome and comfortable you make your guests feel.

You are creating a setting for the Lord to work in the hearts of those you have invited into your home. What an honor it is for you as hostess to be a part of that.

What Treasure a Cookbook!

I'm convinced that every home needs a sturdy foundation, a roof to keep out the rain, a flowerbed and a sampling of good cookbooks. Over the years, I've been the happy recipient of many cookbooks, from the *Silver Palate Cookbook* (recipes from Manhattan's celebrated gourmet food shop) to *Kernel Knowledge*, a real page-turner of 75 standout popcorn recipes. And here's a little secret: You don't always have to cook from your cookbooks. For instant companionship and therapy, you can just curl up and read one like any other good book. Pretty cookbooks are as inviting as an unlicked mixing spoon and always lend a nice decorator touch to the humblest kitchen counter.

It's hard to explain, but a quiet half hour spent poring over mouthwatering pictures and new recipes makes me feel amazingly rejuvenated. I call this the Vicarious Cuisine Cure. I can still go right ahead and make grilled cheese sandwiches for dinner if I want to. When your eyes are burning because you're so tired and you long for your softest pajamas and a good book, Vicarious Cuisine is definitely the way to go.

Thumbed-through cookbooks have a hopeful beauty all their own, revealing that someone cared enough to try their hand at something new, probably with some success. But scribbled-in cookbooks can be heirlooms more precious than the family silver—glowing evidence of a real cook in the house who knows what it is to nourish both body and soul, be it with lobster and wild mushroom salad or a rib-sticking bowl of fragrant bean soup and some cornbread.

There are cookbooks for every season and reason—versions for barbecuers, bakers and appetizer-makers. There are cookbooks for both the reluctant and the eager in the kitchen, the beginner and the accomplished cook, and everyone in between. Plus—just between you and me?—a cookbook is a really, really easy present to wrap.

—Deena Wilson

Planning for Company

Planning is an essential ingredient that contributes to your sense of peace about the wonderful occasion about to take place, and there are some simple and practical things you can do in advance of your guests' arrival to ensure an enjoyable, relaxed evening.

- Choose your menu ahead of time.
- Make a shopping list of all the ingredients you will need to make the food in your recipes.
- Include garnishes in your shopping list. The most common garnish is parsley, but why not try edible flowers or bright, colorful fruit that will complement your entrée? Experiment with some unusual fruit or vegetables; try something like slices of star fruit or using kale leaves. Lemon slices in the water glasses not only add color but also provide a light fresh taste.
- Make a list of any decorative items you might need (candles, napkins, flowers, containers for the centerpiece, etc.).

Appetizers and Condiments

Traditional Christmas Dip
KAY ARTHUR

Ingredients
1 large onion, chopped
1 clove of garlic, chopped, or a dash of garlic powder
1 teaspoon margarine or butter
1 tablespoon chili pepper
1 large can crushed tomatoes
½ pint whipping cream, not whipped
½ teaspoon baking soda
Salt and pepper to taste
1 pound grated American cheese

Directions
1. Sauté onion and garlic in butter or margarine.
2. Add chili pepper and crushed tomatoes.
3. In another pan, heat cream and add baking soda, salt and pepper.
4. When both mixtures are heated, mix together slowly.
5. Stir in grated cheese; continue to stir until the cheese melts.

Suggestion: Serve hot with chips or crackers.

Salmon Ball
JANE HANSEN

Ingredients
8 ounces cream cheese, softened
1 tablespoon lemon juice
3 tablespoons chopped parsley
1 teaspoon horseradish
½ teaspoon onion powder or salt
¼ teaspoon salt
½ teaspoon liquid smoke
1 16-ounce can salmon, drained and flaked
½ cup chopped pecans

Directions
1. Reserve salmon and chopped pecans.
2. Combine all other ingredients with beater or food processor.
3. Flake the salmon and stir into cheese mixture.
4. Chill until you can handle. Roll into a ball or log; then roll in chopped nuts to coat.
5. Chill again until ready to serve.

Let's become "lovers of hospitality" and let our lights shine!

JANE HANSEN

Hot Brie
This is so simple and so addicting! Your guests will love it!
JANE HANSEN

Ingredients
1 block of Brie cheese
Brown sugar
Slivered almonds
¼ cup butter, melted

Directions
1. Place block of Brie in baking pan or casserole dish.
2. Sprinkle with brown sugar and almonds.
3. Melt butter and pour over Brie.
4. Bake at 325° F for 10 to 15 minutes.

Suggestion: Serve with Wheat Thins or other crackers

Hummus (Chickpea Dip)
SUZANNE HINN

Ingredients
2 19-ounce cans of chickpeas (garbanzo beans)
½ cup tahini (sesame seed paste)
4 small cloves of garlic, chopped
Water or lemon juice (optional)
Parsley sprigs
Olive oil

Directions
1. Empty entire contents, including liquid, of cans of chickpeas into medium-sized saucepan.
2. Bring to a boil and simmer on low for 10 minutes with the pan lid on. Set aside to cool.
3. Use a food processor or blender to combine garlic, cooled chickpeas and tahini. Blend until smooth, approximately 2 or 3 minutes, or to desired consistency. If mixture is too thick, it may be thinned with water or lemon juice.
4. Place on platter and garnish with parsley sprigs. Sprinkle olive oil on top.

Suggestion: Serve with torn wedges of pita bread.

Spiced Fruit

As a gift, I can this recipe in quart jars, using a regular canning cooker. You can follow directions from any canning book.

ANNA HAYFORD

Ingredients

Use a variety of canned fruits to equal 2 large cans (a good combination is pears, peaches, pineapple chunks, maraschino cherries and vacuum-packed prunes)

¾ cup brown sugar

½ cup vinegar

1 teaspoon cinnamon

1 teaspoon cloves

Directions

1. Drain syrup from cans of fruit into a pan and add sugar, vinegar and spices.
2. Boil 5 minutes. Add fruit and simmer 10 minutes.
3. Chill and serve.

Crab Dip

This is one of our family's favorites on Christmas Day. Make it ahead; it freezes well.

JANE HANSEN

Ingredients

1 8-ounce package of cream cheese

1 8-ounce can flaked crabmeat

1 garlic clove, finely minced

½ cup mayonnaise

2 teaspoons powdered sugar

2 teaspoons dry mustard

¼ cup sherry

¼ cup slivered almonds, toasted

Salt to taste

Directions

Mix all ingredients well and then heat until bubbly in a casserole dish.

Suggestion: Serve with Wheat Thins or other crackers.

Chutney Dip
Jane Hansen

Ingredients
1 8-ounce package of cream cheese
2 tablespoons cream
3 tablespoons curry powder
Garlic salt
1 teaspoon Worcestershire sauce
1 dash Tabasco sauce
Reese's Chutney Sauce

Directions
1. Blend all ingredients.
2. Top with Reese's Chutney Sauce.

Suggestion: Serve with Wheat Thins.

Savory Appetizer Dip

When God puts on your heart a desire to invite someone over, do so as soon as possible. Think through the event. What will be needed to make the guests feel most welcome and comfortable? Even have some topics of conversation in mind.

Doris Bush

Ingredients
1 envelope of Lipton's Recipe Secrets Vegetable Soup Mix
2 cups sour cream
4 ounces feta or blue cheese, crumbled
½ cup cucumber, seeded and diced
2 tablespoons red onion, chopped
½ teaspoon dried oregano leaves
Pitted ripe olives

Directions
1. Blend all ingredients in a medium-sized bowl.
2. Chill.
3. Garnish with pitted ripe olives.

Suggestion: Serve with pita bread and/or fresh raw vegetables.

Blueberry Syrup

This syrup is great over pancakes or ice cream.

SANDRA WEZOWICZ

Ingredients
8 cups blueberries
3 cups sugar
1 cup corn syrup
¼ cup lemon juice

Directions
1. Crush berries and bring to a boil over medium heat.
2. Pour through a strainer to yield 3 to 4 cups of juice.
3. Combine juice with sugar, corn syrup and lemon juice and boil for 1 minute.

Tip: This syrup may be canned using the water bath method.

Honey Granola

It burns very quickly; keep an eye on it.

DENISE FRANGIPANE

Ingredients
6 cups oats, quick or old fashioned
1 cup sunflower seeds
1 cup almonds, sliced, chopped or slivered
1 cup coconut, flaked or shredded
1 cup dates
1 teaspoon cinnamon
2 teaspoons vanilla
½ cup canola oil
½ cup honey

Directions
1. Spray two large baking pans with Pam.
2. Mix all dry ingredients and set aside.
3. Mix liquid ingredients together and add to dry ingredients.
4. Pour granola mixture into the prepared baking pans.
5. Bake at 300° F for 45 minutes, stirring every 15 minutes.

Hot Pepper Jelly
CAROLYN JONES

Ingredients

2 cups bell peppers, any color, finely chopped
⅔ cup hot (jalapeño) peppers, finely chopped
2⅔ cups cider vinegar
4⅔ cups sugar
3 teaspoons Pomona's Universal Pectin powder
4 teaspoons calcium water (calcium included in
    pectin package)

Directions

1. Wash and sterilize jars. Let stand in hot water until ready
   to use.
2. Heat sealing lids in water (just below boiling point.)
   Let stand in water until ready to use.
3. Be sure to wear rubber gloves when handling hot peppers,
   and avoid touching your eyes.
4. Measure chopped peppers and cider vinegar into a large
   nonaluminum kettle and bring to a rolling boil.
5. Add pectin and sugar to boiling mixture and stir vigorously
   for 1 to 2 minutes to dissolve. (Pomona's Universal Pectin is
   a low-methozyl pectin that doesn't require sugar to set. It is
   available in most health food stores. One package will make
   almost 16 cups of jam.)
6. Add calcium water and stir well.
7. Fill jars to within ½ inch of top. Wipe rims and seal. Process
   in water bath canner for 5 minutes. Remove from water and
   cool. Check lids for seal.

Suggestions: Serve jelly with cream cheese and crackers, or use as
a glaze to brush over roasting meat, fish or poultry.

Much of the enjoyment of

having guests is in preparations

that will make them feel special.

I like to put a place card at each

place; then I add a favor, like a

small basket with mints or

perhaps an angel or tiny book.

On occasion I have also written

a short special note with

a Scripture verse and put one

at each place.

MARY LANCE SISK

Banana Crush

A delicious summer beverage enjoyed by both children and adults.

WANDA HANSEN

Ingredients

6 cups water
2½ cups sugar
2 8-ounce cans frozen orange juice
1 8-ounce can frozen lemonade
5 ripe bananas
1 46-ounce can unsweetened pineapple juice
4 quarts 7 UP

Directions

1. Heat the water and sugar together until the sugar is dissolved.
2. Mix in a blender the frozen juices and bananas.
3. Mix banana juice mixture with the sugar water and pineapple juice.
4. Freeze.
5. Before serving, partially thaw the fruit mixture and mix with 4 quarts of 7 UP.

White Caramel Corn

WANDA HANSEN

Ingredients

⅞ cup (1¾ sticks) butter
1½ cups sugar
½ cup white Karo syrup
1 tablespoon vanilla
3 to 4 gallons popped popcorn

Directions

1. Cook butter, sugar and syrup at medium boil for 6 to 8 minutes until the soft ball stage.
2. Remove from heat, add vanilla and stir.
3. Pour syrup over popped popcorn and toss to coat thoroughly.
4. Spread in a greased shallow pan and bake in a 225° F oven for 30 to 40 minutes. Stir occasionally.
5. Pour popcorn out onto counter to cool. Store in airtight containers.

Suggestions: If you like really warm "sticky" caramel corn, then do not bake. To make it look festive, you can add food coloring when you add the vanilla.

Extending the Invitation

It's important for your invitation to match the mood of your get-together—different types of gatherings call for different types of invitations.

- Written invitations are most appropriate for more formal gatherings. Guests will have a record of when and where the party is, and any extra details are down on paper. Include your phone number and an RSVP request, so you'll know how many guests to expect. And remember, "written" doesn't mean boring. Let your invitations reflect your personality.
- For casual gatherings, a telephone call will suffice. You'll get immediate responses and have a chance to chat with friends. Just remember to try to call everyone on the same day—that way no one feels left out.
- For informal gatherings, try e-mailing invitations. The Internet gives you access to lots of fun and different electronic cards.
- For open houses, try staggering the invitations. Invite business associates and acquaintances for the first few hours; then invite your friends to close the party. This way no one gets left out, your house never gets too full, and you can relax with friends before the evening is over.

Breads

Source of Life

Whether it be the pita bread of Middle Eastern nations, the Santi bread of West Africa, the wonderful breads of Europe or the tortillas of Latin America, bread is a food generally regarded as the sustenance of life.

In the Bible, bread signifies satisfaction. Jesus said, "I am the bread of life. He who comes to Me shall never hunger" (John 6:35); what Jesus is actually saying to us is "I am the true bread that satisfies." As the bread of life, He is to the soul what bread is to the body. He alone can nourish and give life. He alone can give to us the deep inner satisfaction for which our soul longs. In giving us Christ, God has provided our single greatest need—life! In Christ we not only receive the gift of eternal life but also the source of daily life and satisfaction.

Pumpkin Bread
Diane Moder

Ingredients

2⅔ cups sugar
⅔ cup butter or margarine
4 eggs, beaten
1 16-ounce can pumpkin
⅔ cup water
3⅓ cups flour
½ teaspoon baking powder
2 teaspoons soda
½ teaspoon salt
1 teaspoon cinnamon
½ teaspoon cloves

⅔ cup walnuts, chopped
⅔ cup dates, chopped

Directions

1. Cream sugar and butter until light and fluffy.
2. Mix together eggs, pumpkin and water and stir into creamed mixture.
3. Mix dry ingredients and stir into pumpkin mixture.
4. Stir in nuts and dates.
5. Bake in two well-greased bread pans in a 350° F oven for 1 hour and 15 minutes to 1 hour and 25 minutes. Test with a toothpick in the center to see if they are done.

Tip: If wrapped in aluminum foil, they will keep in the refrigerator for several weeks, or they may be frozen.

Simplest Yeast Rolls Ever

When Jane comes for dinner at our house, she always requests these rolls. . . actually she begs! We are always glad to have an opportunity to bless her. These rolls are so easy to make, my kids make them for me quite often.
Wanda Hansen

Ingredients

½ cup honey or sugar
2 teaspoons salt
1 cup boiling water
1 cup cold water
2 packages yeast
½ cup oil
2 eggs
3 cups white flour
3 cups whole wheat flour

Directions

1. Combine honey, salt, boiling water and cold water.
2. Add yeast, oil, eggs and flour.
3. Mix to make a soft dough.
4. Let rise until double (about 2 hours) in bulk. Punch dough down.
5. Let rise again. Punch dough down.
6. Shape as dinner rolls or cinnamon rolls. Place in greased baking pan, let rise again, and bake at 375° F, until golden brown.

Banana Crumb Muffins
DENISE FRANGIPANE

Muffin Ingredients

¾ cup whole wheat pastry flour
¾ cup plus 1 tablespoon white flour
1 teaspoon baking powder
1 teaspoon baking soda
½ teaspoon salt
1 egg, slightly beaten
⅔ cup honey
3 ripe bananas
½ cup applesauce or butter

Topping Ingredients

1 tablespoon flour
⅓ cup date sugar, brown sugar or Sucanat
⅓ teaspoon cinnamon
1 tablespoon butter, chilled

Directions

1. In a large bowl mix dry ingredients.
2. Combine egg, honey, bananas and applesauce, and mix well.
3. Stir into dry ingredients, just until moistened.
4. Fill greased muffin cups ¾ full.
5. For topping: Combine flour, sugar and cinnamon. Cut in chilled butter and mix until crumbly.
6. Sprinkle over muffins.
7. Bake at 325° F for 20 to 25 minutes. Test with a toothpick to be sure they are done.

Makes 12 muffins

Just 15 minutes a day will bring order to your spiritual life or your physical home. Clean one drawer, one cupboard, etc. each day and you will soon be in perfect order.

PATTI MCGINNIS

Mary Tucker's Fried Biscuits

When I was growing up, this recipe of my mother's was a special treat served to visitors in our home in Peoga, Indiana.

MARILYN TUCKER QUAYLE

Ingredients

1 package yeast
½ cup warm water
2 cups milk, scalded
3 rounded tablespoons sugar
3 tablespoons margarine
1 tablespoon salt
6 cups flour
Crisco shortening

Directions

1. Dissolve yeast in water in small bowl and set aside for about 5 minutes.
2. Mix all ingredients together in the order they appear, reserving ½ cup flour to use while kneading.
3. Knead the dough for 5 minutes. Cover and let rise in a greased bowl in a warm place until double in bulk.
4. Punch dough down and knead again and let rise a second time until double in bulk.
5. Punch dough down and gently knead for 1 minute.
6. On lightly floured board, roll dough to ¾ of an inch thick. Cut with a donut or biscuit cutter.
7. In a fryer or saucepan, heat 3 inches of Crisco shortening.
8. Gently ease biscuits into hot oil, turning as they cook to brown evenly.
9. Remove biscuits when browned and place on absorbent toweling and keep warm.

Suggestion: Serve warm with apple butter.

When I entertain large groups and want everything to be ready at the same time, I write out my menu and prepare a time schedule, starting with my serving time and working it out in reverse. On my schedule I write down what time I need to start cooking each menu item. This way nothing is forgotten and everything is ready at the right time—with my schedule prepared, my guests are often eager to help, too.

CAROLYN JONES

Blueberry Muffins
SANDRA WEZOWICZ

Ingredients

1¾ cup flour
2 teaspoons baking powder
¼ teaspoon salt
¾ cup sugar, plus a little extra for sprinkling
½ cup milk
1 egg
¼ cup margarine, melted
1 cup blueberries

Directions

1. Sift together all dry ingredients.
2. Add the milk, egg and melted margarine to the dry ingredients.
3. Fold in berries (if using frozen berries, do not thaw first).
4. Fill greased or paper-lined muffin cups ⅔ full.
5. Sprinkle with extra sugar.
6. Bake 25 minutes at 400° F.

Magic Marshmallow Puffs
JANE HANSEN

Ingredients

16 marshmallows
¼ cup butter or margarine, melted
¼ cup sugar mixed with 1 teaspoon cinnamon
2 cans Pillsbury Crescent Rolls
Powdered sugar glaze
Nuts (optional)

Directions

1. Preheat oven to 375° F.
2. Dip marshmallows in melted butter or margarine.
3. Roll in sugar and cinnamon mixture.
4. Wrap crescent triangle around each marshmallow, covering the marshmallow completely by squeezing the edges of the dough tightly to seal.
5. Dip the covered marshmallows in the butter or margarine and place in muffin pans.
6. Place pan on foil and bake for 10 to 15 minutes until golden brown. (They tend to bubble over the edges of the pan.)
7. Cool slightly and drizzle with powdered sugar glaze. Sprinkle with nuts, if desired.

Serves 8

Popovers
JEAN VANDENBOS

Ingredients

6 eggs
2 cups milk
6 tablespoons butter, melted
2 cups flour
1 teaspoon salt
½ cup chopped pecans (optional)

Makes 8 large popovers
Suggestion: Serve with butter and marmalade.

Directions

1. Preheat oven to 375° F.
2. Beat eggs slightly, and then add milk and melted butter.
3. Add flour and salt.
4. Do this much the night before and chill batter in a covered container.
5. Pour into 6-ounce Pyrex baking cups to within ¼ inch of the top.
6. Sprinkle with 1 tablespoon pecans (this is optional, but a nice touch).
7. Bake for 1 hour (DO NOT PEEK).

Applesauce Muffins
ZEE JONES

Ingredients

⅓ cup shortening
1 cup sugar
1 egg
1 cup applesauce
2 cups flour
1 teaspoon soda
1 teaspoon baking powder
½ teaspoon cream of tartar
½ teaspoon salt
½ teaspoon cloves
1 teaspoon cinnamon
½ cup raisins
Walnuts

Directions

1. Cream together shortening, sugar and egg; stir in applesauce.
2. Combine dry ingredients and stir into creamed mixture.
3. Carefully stir in raisins and nuts.
4. Spoon into prepared muffin cups.
5. Bake at 325° F for 30 minutes.

Orange Rolls
CAROLYN JONES

Ingredients

4½ cups all-purpose flour
1 package dry yeast
1 cup milk
½ cup granulated sugar
½ teaspoon salt
3 tablespoons butter or margarine
3 eggs
6 tablespoons butter, softened
½ cup granulated sugar
1½ teaspoons orange peel, shredded
1½ cups powdered sugar, sifted
2 to 3 tablespoons fresh-squeezed orange juice

Directions

1. In a large mixer bowl, combine 2 cups of the flour and the yeast.
2. Heat milk, ½ cup sugar, salt and 3 tablespoons butter until warm (115° to 120°), stirring to melt butter.
3. Add the liquid mixture to the dry mixture and then add the eggs.
4. Beat with mixer on low speed for ½ minute, scraping bowl.
5. Beat with mixer at high speed for 3 minutes. Stir in enough remaining flour to make a moderately soft dough. Knead on a floured surface until the dough is smooth (3 to 5 minutes).
6. Place dough in a greased bowl; turn over, cover with a cloth and let it rise until doubled (1 to 1½ hours). Punch dough down and cover; let rest 10 minutes.
7. Divide dough into two parts and roll each into a 12x8-inch rectangle. Combine 6 tablespoons butter, ½ cup sugar and orange peel. Spread the mixture over the dough. Roll up, starting with the long side; pinch seams to seal. Cut each roll into 12 slices and place cut side down in the greased cup of a muffin pan, or arrange in a rectangular or square baking pan.
8. Cover and let rise for about 1½ hours. Bake at 375° F for 15 to 20 minutes.
9. Remove immediately from pan. Combine powdered sugar and orange juice for glaze and drizzle over the rolls while still warm.

Makes approximately 24 rolls

Swedish Cinnamon Rolls

On Christmas Eve morning I deliver a dozen of these cinnamon rolls to several special people.
It has become a tradition anticipated by all who have ever eaten them. One thing that makes them easy
is that they are mixed at night and shaped and baked in the morning.

CAROLYN JONES

Ingredients

½ cup shortening
½ cup butter
1 cup sugar
1 cup unseasoned mashed potatoes
½ cup potato water
1 package of dry yeast or 1 ounce fresh cake yeast
½ cup warm water
1 cup scalded milk, cooled
2 rounded teaspoons salt
2 eggs
7 cups flour (a little more flour can be used,
   but this is a very soft dough)
¼ pound softened butter
1 pound brown sugar
Cinnamon to taste
Powdered sugar
Water
Vanilla

Directions

1. Mix together shortening and butter, sugar, mashed potatoes, potato water, yeast dissolved in water, milk, salt, eggs and flour.
2. Knead 10 minutes. Dough will be soft and somewhat sticky. Do not add more than ½ cup flour while kneading.
3. Let stand overnight in a large greased bowl covered with plastic wrap and a cloth.
4. The next day, punch down dough and roll out half of it to about a 16 x 20-inch rectangle. Spread with half the butter and brown sugar. Sprinkle with cinnamon to taste. Repeat with remaining dough.
5. Roll up dough and cut into 1-inch slices. (A piece of thread works nicely to cut. Place thread under roll of dough, about one inch from end. Bring ends over the top of the roll, cross and tighten; the thread will cut through the dough and not crush the slices.) Place slices cut side down on greased baking pans.
6. Cover with a cloth and let rise 1 hour in a warm place or until at least double in size.
7. Bake at 350° F for 15 to 20 minutes.
8. While still warm, drizzle with a thin glaze of powdered sugar, water and vanilla.

Makes 36 rolls

Hosting Children in Your Home

Whatever the occasion, be sure to cater to any "little" guests you might be expecting. Consider having a children's table just for them—and make their dining experience fun!

- Think ahead to the area where children will be and remove anything so valuable you would be horrified if it broke. (This helps you to not worry and helps parents to not have to say no all the time.)
- Consider the children's likes and dislikes and plan to have at least two foods they will most likely enjoy eating. (Ask parents ahead of time, if you need suggestions.)
- Plan a fun activity or two to keep kids amused while adults visit. You might try sidewalk chalk for drawing on patios and driveways, bubbles to blow, inexpensive stickers to arrange on paper, or play dough and cookie cutters. An older child might enjoy using a disposable camera.

- Have a few finger-food snacks in baggies ready for kids who are hungry when they first arrive and can't wait until the meal is ready.
- Keep a box of safe, clean toys (one or two for each age level) to offer children who are visitors. You can purchase these from thrift stores or at garage sales, or keep some of your own children's toys for future use. You could also ask parents to bring along a toy or game their children enjoy.
- Cover the tabletop with a sheet of butcher paper, inexpensive craft paper or paper placemats and provide crayons for kids to color.
- If you're eating outdoors, let the children decorate the tabletop with leaves, twigs and flower petals.
- If children will be seated at a table, think ahead to what children will sit on and either get appropriate seating or ask parents to bring along what is needed (high chair, booster seat, etc.).

Soups

Hospitality—Soup for the Soul

The root word for "hospitality" is "hospital." When we think of a hospital, we think of a shelter—a refuge where the ill or injured can come for care with the objective of being restored to health and wholeness again.

Hospitality can have that same healing effect. I remember a time when I was struggling and in much emotional pain. A friend invited me to lunch. When I walked in she had a fire in the fireplace, soft music playing, candles burning and a simple but lovely lunch table set. Just the warmth of the atmosphere began to minister to my hurting heart. As we ate, shared and then prayed together, I thought of the words of Jesus when He said to Zacchaeus, "I must stay at your house" (Luke 19:5). As this personal encounter took place, Zacchaeus's heart was turned toward God in a new way, just as my heart was also touched anew through the hospitality of my friend and I realized His love for me in a deeper way.

Chicken Tortilla Soup
CAROL TORRANCE

Ingredients

3 to 4 boneless chicken breasts
Water to cover chicken
2 cups chicken broth
1 48-ounce Spicy V-8
½ purple onion, chopped
½ green pepper, chopped
1 8-ounce can tomato sauce
1 8-ounce can diced tomatoes
Tortilla chips
Cheddar or mozzarella cheese, grated

Directions

1. Boil chicken breasts in water until tender, drain and reserve 2 cups broth.
2. Cut chicken into small pieces.
3. Combine chicken with remaining ingredients in a crock-pot and cook until vegetables are tender.
4. Break tortilla chips in the bottom of each serving bowl and pour soup over chips.
5. Top with grated cheese.

Creamy Chicken Noodle Soup
CAROLYN JONES

Ingredients

8 cups chicken broth or bouillon
1½ cups milk, divided
¾ cup carrots, quartered lengthwise and thinly sliced
½ cup celery, sliced
½ cup green pepper, chopped
⅓ cup onion, chopped
1 clove garlic, minced
½ teaspoon dried marjoram leaves, crushed
½ teaspoon salt
½ teaspoon pepper
2 cups cooked chicken, diced
6 ounces medium egg noodles, uncooked
¼ cup flour
2 tablespoons butter or margarine

Directions

1. In a 6-quart kettle, stir together broth or bouillon, 1 cup milk, carrots, celery, green pepper, onion, garlic, marjoram, salt and pepper.
2. Over medium heat, cook for 20 minutes or until vegetables are crisp-tender.
3. Add chicken and noodles. Cook for 10 to 12 minutes or until noodles are almost tender.
4. In a cup, stir together remaining ½ cup milk and the flour until smooth. Stir into soup mixture.
5. Stirring over medium-high heat, bring to a boil and boil until slightly thickened. Stir in butter or margarine until melted.

Serves 8
Suggestion: Serve with toasted, buttered French bread.

Baked Minestrone Soup

A hearty soup, good for a cold winter day—easy to prepare ahead.

CAROL GREENWOOD

Ingredients

2 pounds beef stew meat, or a beef roast, cubed
1 cup chopped onion
1 teaspoon minced garlic
1 teaspoon salt
¼ teaspoon cayenne pepper
2 tablespoons olive oil
2 cans beef broth
2½ cans water
1 15-ounce can kidney beans
1 large can tomatoes
1 cup seashell macaroni
2 cups sliced zucchini
1½ teaspoons Italian seasoning
1 can pitted olives
¾ cup Parmesan cheese

Directions

1. Combine beef, onion, garlic, salt and pepper and olive oil in a Dutch oven. Brown uncovered in 400° F oven for 30 to 40 minutes, stirring occasionally. Reduce heat to 350° F.
2. Add beef broth and water. Cover and bake 1 hour.
3. Stir in remaining ingredients.
4. Top with Parmesan cheese; bake an additional 45 minutes.

Serves 6 to 8

Salmon Chowder

We traditionally serve this for Christmas Eve.

WANDA HANSEN

Ingredients

1 16-ounce can salmon
¼ cup onion, chopped
¼ cup celery, chopped
¼ cup butter, melted
2 tablespoons flour
4 cups milk
1 cup raw potatoes, diced
1 cup tomato juice
1½ teaspoons salt

Directions

1. Drain and flake salmon, reserving liquid.
2. In a saucepan, cook onion and celery in butter until tender.
3. Blend in flour, add milk and potatoes, and cook until potatoes are tender.
4. In another saucepan heat tomato juice and salt.
5. Combine both mixtures; add salmon and its liquid.
6. Heat to serving temperature.

Seattle Style Clam Chowder
(Specialty of the former Seattle Style Restaurant)
CAROLYN JONES

Ingredients

3 pounds small red potatoes, scrubbed and diced
Water to cover potatoes
4 tablespoons butter
1 large carrot, peeled and diced
3 large stalks celery, washed and diced
1 medium onion, peeled and diced
½ pound bacon, cooked until crisp, crumbled
1 clove garlic, peeled and crushed
1 teaspoon black pepper
¼ teaspoon Tabasco sauce
1 teaspoon dried dill, crushed
1 teaspoon dried thyme, crushed
1 large bay leaf
1 teaspoon basil
3 6.5-ounce cans chopped clams, with juice
2 cups half-and-half or whipping cream

Directions

1. Bring water to a boil in a large pan, add the potatoes, and cook until tender.
2. Drain, reserving 1 cup of the cooking water. Set potatoes and water aside.
3. In a 6-quart pan, heat the butter over medium heat. Add the carrot and cook until tender, about 8 minutes. Add the celery and cook until tender, about 5 minutes. Stir in the onion and bacon and cook until the vegetables are tender, about 5 minutes.
4. Add the garlic, pepper, Tabasco, dill, thyme, bay leaf and basil, sautéing for about 3 minutes to blend. Stir in the clams with the juice; bring to a boil, stirring constantly. Add the potatoes, potato water and half-and-half or whipping cream. Bring just to a boil, reduce the heat, and simmer for 20 minutes.
5. Cool slightly and refrigerate overnight to blend the flavors.
6. Reheat gently before serving.

Serves 8

A large pot of soup and crusty rolls with a simple dessert are a great informal meal to enjoy with friends. The best thing about soup is that it can be made the day before because it gets better as the flavors blend—and you'll enjoy entertaining that much more!

CAROLYN JONES

Egg Drop Soup
CAROLYNNE CHUNG

Ingredients

1 whole chicken (3 to 4 pounds)
1 carrot, cut in large chunks
1 onion, quartered
1 stalk celery, cut in large chunks
Water to cover
2 tablespoons cornstarch
1 egg
Scallions, sliced

Directions

1. Place chicken and vegetables in a pot and cover with water.
2. Cover and simmer on very low heat for 1 hour.
3. Remove chicken from stock. Cool and use for salads, casseroles, etc.
4. Discard the vegetables.
5. Put 4 cups of chicken stock in smaller pot.
6. Stir small amount of stock into cornstarch. Then add mixture to stock in pot and stir while heating till it begins to thicken.
7. Slowly pour in 1 beaten egg and stir gently for a moment.
8. Remove soup from heat. Pour into bowls and garnish with sliced scallions

Serves 4

Authentic Chinese cuisine is as important to my Chinese-American husband as shortbread and maple syrup is to me, a Canadian. Food is an important link to our families of origin and the memories of family get-togethers. When our daughters come home from college on breaks there are always certain recipes that come out of the file. They want the recipes they remember from their years at home, not new ones I have tried since they left!

CAROLYNNE CHUNG

Taco Soup
CAROLYN JONES

Ingredients

¾ pound ground beef
2 tablespoons chopped onion
¼ cup prepared taco sauce
1 8-ounce can stewed tomatoes
1 8-ounce can kidney beans, undrained
1 7-ounce can whole kernel corn, undrained
1-1½ teaspoons chili powder
¼ teaspoon garlic salt
6 tablespoons cheddar cheese, shredded
3 tablespoons dairy sour cream

Directions

1. In a large saucepan, brown ground beef and onion; drain.
2. Add taco sauce, tomatoes, beans, corn, chili powder and garlic salt; mix well.
3. Bring to a boil, and simmer covered for 15 minutes.
4. Sprinkle 2 tablespoons shredded cheese and a tablespoon of sour cream on each serving.

Serves 3

Cream of Corn Soup
JOANNE MECKSTROTH

Ingredients

2 strips bacon, finely chopped
2 teaspoons onion, finely chopped
2 cups corn, frozen or fresh
2 tablespoons butter
2 tablespoons flour
2 cups milk
1 teaspoon salt
½ teaspoon pepper
2 cups light cream

Directions

1. Fry chopped bacon until crisp; add onion and sauté until soft.
2. Put corn through a food chopper, add to onion and bacon, and cook until it begins to brown.
3. Add butter and then the flour.
4. Cook on medium-low heat for 3 minutes.
5. Add milk, salt and pepper and cook until thickened.
6. Add cream; heat until smooth.

Serves 6

Mimi's Quick and Easy Potato Soup
THETUS TENNEY

Ingredients

1 small package of frozen hash brown potatoes

2 cans of chicken broth and one can of water, or 2 cubes
   of chicken bouillon with 4 cups of water

Salt and pepper to taste

1 teaspoon dried parsley

½ teaspoon onion flakes, or onion, minced

½ teaspoon celery salt

1 small can evaporated milk or whole milk, if desired

1 cup instant mashed potatoes

1 can cheese soup

Directions

1. Combine hash brown potatoes with broth and water.
2. Add salt, pepper, parsley, onion flakes and celery salt.
3. Bring to a boil, reduce heat and cook until well done.
4. Gradually stir in milk.
5. Sprinkle instant potatoes on top and whisk into mix.
6. Simmer to thicken. Add cheese soup. (Milk and instant potatoes can be adjusted for desired thickness.)

Serves 6 to 8

Suggestion: Serve with hot crusty rolls or grilled cheese sandwiches.

Sauerkraut Soup
This is a great crock-pot dinner. Just add the sauerkraut when you get home and it's ready.
WANDA HANSEN

Ingredients

1 pound pork, chopped and browned

1 pound Polish sausage, sliced and browned

1 medium onion, chopped

1 cup carrots, finely chopped

1 cup potatoes, diced

1 cup tart apple, chopped

2 or 3 cloves garlic, crushed

2 tablespoons brown sugar

1 teaspoon caraway seed

½ teaspoon ginger

1 teaspoon ground cloves

4 to 5 cups water

1 small jar sauerkraut

Directions

1. Combine all ingredients except sauerkraut and bring to a boil.
2. Turn heat to medium and cook until vegetables are tender.
3. Add sauerkraut and cook for an additional 15 minutes.
4. Serve hot.

Savory Summer Soup
CAROLYN JONES

Ingredients

4 medium-sized zucchini, sliced
1 green pepper, seeded and sliced
3 medium-sized onions, sliced
2 large garlic cloves, sliced
4 tablespoons butter
2 tablespoons fresh thyme, chopped
Salt and white pepper
6 cups chicken broth
1 cup heavy cream
Fresh chives, finely cut, or fresh parsley, chopped

Directions

1. In a heavy pot, sauté three of the sliced zucchini with the green pepper, onions and garlic in 3 tablespoons of butter over very low heat.
2. Cook, stirring often, for about 10 minutes, or until the vegetables are tender but have not browned.
3. Add the thyme; salt and pepper to taste.
4. Stir in the chicken broth and simmer uncovered for 15 minutes.
5. Sauté the remaining zucchini in 1 tablespoon of butter until it is barely tender and still bright green. This should take about 3 minutes. Stir and watch closely that it doesn't overcook and become mushy.
6. Turn the sautéed zucchini out onto a plate to cool quickly. Reserve.
7. Cool the vegetable broth mixture slightly and puree it in a blender or food mill.
8. In a bowl, stir the cream into the puree and add the sliced, sautéed zucchini. Adjust the seasonings—the soup should be rather highly seasoned, as chilling reduces flavors. Chill for 24 hours and garnish the soup with a scattering of fresh chives or parsley.

Serves 6 to 8

Lovely, formal meals are a beautiful occasion, but simple settings and down-home meals seem to establish comfortable relationships more quickly. A good hearty soup with crusty bread and a simple dessert served at the kitchen table truly allow people to make themselves at home. A kitchen meal can still be attractive and say to your guests that they are special. Colorful placemats and napkins with a simple vase of flowers, a small potted plant or a pretty ceramic piece makes a simple but nice setting.

THETUS TENNEY

Creating a Welcoming Ambiance

Look with fresh eyes at key areas in your home that guests will be seeing. Don't be afraid to try new things. For example:

- Consider what would bring that special touch to the entryway, bathrooms, kitchen, conversation areas, living room and dining room—touches that say "I am so glad you came!"
- Make sure you have fresh hand towels and soap.
- A dinner party doesn't always have to be served in the dining room. If it is a more casual get-together and you have a spacious kitchen or family room, plan to have your guests gather there.
- Rather than using a tablecloth, try using a colorful quilt, a piece of fabric or even netting to bring a different feel to your table setting.
- Follow a particular theme for the evening and let your decorations and your choice of food echo that theme.

While you want the glow of many candles to fill your entertaining area, it is important to observe the lighting in other areas as well.

- Be sure that conversational areas are well lit. Place individual lamps so that the light beckons people to come and sit down.
- Arrange furniture in such a way that people can easily chat with one another; small groupings are nice.
- Make sure your outside entryway is well lit, so people can see your house address and easily find their way to the door.
- If the dining area faces an outside window, add some kind of lighting outside the window to draw the outside beauty into your room. You can use something as simple and easy as tiki torches or place outside lights close to trees or shrubs for special effect.
- Select music that will help set the mood for the evening. Lovely, soft background music brings an almost instant sense of peace to the atmosphere. Choose a type of music and adjust the level of the sound so that your guests will not have to compete with the music as they talk with each other.

Salads and Side Dishes

Poppy Seed Citrus Salad
GRETCHEN FINCH MAHONEY

Salad Ingredients

1 head romaine lettuce, torn into bite-sized pieces
1 10-ounce can grapefruit sections, drained
2 small cans mandarin oranges, drained
1 large ripe avocado
½ cup coconut, flaked

Dressing Ingredients

½ cup cider vinegar
¾ cup canola oil
½ cup sugar
1 teaspoon salt
1 tablespoon poppy seeds
2 teaspoons dry mustard
1½ teaspoon paprika
2 teaspoons dry minced onions

Directions

1. Combine all dressing ingredients in blender or shake in a jar with a tight lid.
2. Put all salad ingredients, except coconut, into salad bowl.
3. Add just enough dressing to moisten and toss.
4. Serve coconut in a small bowl on the side.

Frozen Fruit Salad
BARBARA JAMES

Ingredients

1 pint sour cream
Juice of 2 lemons
1 cup sugar
1 small jar maraschino cherries, whole or cut in pieces
1 large can crushed pineapple
1 cup nuts, chopped
2 bananas, mashed
Lettuce

Directions

1. Mix together all ingredients.
2. Freeze in paper baking cups to make individual servings.
3. Remove paper baking cups and arrange each salad on a bed of lettuce.

Fruited Chicken Macadamia Salad
VIRGINIA OTIS

Ingredients
1 cup Macadamia nuts, toasted, plus extras for sprinkling
¼ cup mayonnaise
¼ cup sour cream
2 tablespoons green onions with tops, finely chopped
1 teaspoon lemon juice
1½ cups chicken, cooked and diced
1 cup green seedless grapes
Salt
Pepper
Crisp lettuce

Directions
1. Toast Macadamia nuts by sprinkling nuts on a baking sheet and lightly browning them in a moderate (325° F) oven for about 4 minutes; stir or shake occasionally.
2. Combine mayonnaise, sour cream, onion and lemon juice; toss gently with chicken, grapes and toasted nuts.
3. Season with salt and pepper.
4. Arrange on lettuce leaf on a serving platter or on individual plates.
5. Sprinkle with additional toasted Macadamia nuts.

Serves 4

Cranberry Jell-O
This is a wonderful complement to dinner and is so good with poultry or pork.
JANE HANSEN

Ingredients
1 cup fresh cranberries, ground (measure before grinding)
2 3-ounce packages cherry Jell-O
2 cups boiling water
1 cup cold pineapple juice (juice from canned pineapple plus water to make a cup)
½ cup sugar
2 tablespoons lemon juice, fresh or bottled
1 9-ounce can pineapple tidbits
¾ cup celery
½ fresh orange, chopped
½ teaspoon orange peel, grated
Walnuts, chopped

Directions
1. Grind fresh cranberries.
2. Dissolve Jell-O in boiling water; add pineapple juice.
3. Add sugar and lemon juice; stir until sugar is dissolved.
4. Cool Jell-O and add pineapple, celery, cranberries, orange, orange peel and walnuts.
5. Pour into a serving bowl and chill to set.

Hot Chinese Chicken Salad

During the 40 years Paul and I have been married, the Lord has taught me a number of things about having people in our home to share Jesus' love and be a lighthouse! The main thing is to always keep it simple . . . nice and special, but simple! For this recipe I like to have all the ingredients ready in small bowls. While we visit in the kitchen area, I can pull it all together. Everything is extremely casual and the salad preparation time becomes sort of a nonthreatening sharing time.

JEANNIE CEDAR

Ingredients

3 to 4 whole chicken breasts, cut in chunks
¼ cup cornstarch
¼ cup oil
1 4-ounce can sliced, or ¼ pound fresh, mushrooms
1 4-ounce can water chestnuts, sliced
1 cup celery, sliced diagonally
¼ cup soy sauce
2 large tomatoes, cut into wedges
Salt
Pepper
Lettuce, shredded
Baby spinach

Directions

1. Cut chicken in chunks and roll in cornstarch.
2. Lightly brown chicken in oil.
3. Add mushrooms, water chestnuts, and celery.
4. Stir in soy sauce and simmer 4 minutes.
5. Toss all of the above ingredients together with tomato wedges, salt, pepper, lettuce and spinach.

Two ideas I have utilized in the area of hospitality:

small potted plants on the table that are later given as a gift to each lady present, and

Scripture promises that bless, rolled up like small scrolls, tied with ribbon and arranged in a

crystal bowl for each person to draw at the end of the meal.

VIRGINIA OTIS

Corned Beef Luncheon Salad

MYSTEL WILLAMSON

Ingredients

1 3-ounce package lemon Jell-O
1½ cups water
1 cup mayonnaise
½ can corned beef, flaked or shredded
1 cup celery, chopped
½ cup green pepper, chopped
1 tablespoon onion, chopped
1 teaspoon vinegar

Directions

1. Make Jell-O with 1½ cups water. When slightly set, beat with mixer until fluffy.
2. Add mayonnaise and beat well.
3. Fold in all other ingredients. Pour into a mold and chill until set.

Fanciful Pretzel Salad

This is one of my favorites. Whenever I have taken the time to make this beautiful salad, it has been a smashing success with fancy party-goers, and a favorite of my whole family at birthdays and holidays.

EVELYN CHRISTENSON

Ingredients

12 ounces cream cheese
½ cup milk
1¼ cups sugar
2⅔ cups pretzels, coarsely crushed
⅜ pound (1½ sticks) margarine, melted
9 ounces (or less) Cool Whip
1 6-ounce package strawberry Jell-O
2 cups canned pineapple juice, heated
3 cups strawberries with juice, fresh or frozen
   (if fresh, sweeten to taste and mash slightly)

Directions

1. Mix cream cheese and milk; blend in sugar and set aside.
2. Mix crushed pretzels and melted margarine and press into 9x13-inch baking dish.
3. Bake at 400° F for 10 minutes.
4. Spread cream cheese mixture over warm (not hot) pretzels.
5. Spread Cool Whip over the cream cheese mixture and chill.
6. Dissolve Jell-O in hot pineapple juice; cool to room temperature.
7. Add strawberries and let gel partially.
8. Pour partially set Jell-O over the chilled ingredients and refrigerate to set. Keeps well for two days.

Serves 12

Creamy Fruit Ring
NANCY MCGUIRK

Ingredients
2 cups boiling liquid (water or syrup from fruit)
1 6-ounce package raspberry gelatin
1 pint raspberry sherbet
1 11-ounce can mandarin orange segments, drained
1 13½-ounce can pineapple chunks, drained
1 cup flaked coconut
1 cup miniature marshmallows
1 cup sour cream

Directions
1. Pour boiling liquid over gelatin in bowl, stirring until gelatin is dissolved.
2. Stir in raspberry sherbet until melted.
3. Pour into a 4-cup ring mold and chill until firm.
4. Combine mandarin oranges, pineapple, coconut and marshmallows.
5. Fold in sour cream and chill at least 3 hours.
6. Just before serving, remove gelatin from mold and fill center of unmolded salad with fruit mixture.

Serves 6 to 8

Fruit Salad
MARILYN TUCKER QUAYLE

Salad Ingredients
Apple pieces
Melon balls
Orange sections
Grapefruit sections
Strawberries
Pear pieces
Bananas, sliced
Grapes, red and green seedless
Coconut, shredded
Nuts, chopped
Lettuce
Kiwi

Orange Vanilla Dressing Ingredients
1 cup vanilla yogurt
2 tablespoons orange juice concentrate

Directions
1. Prepare 6 cups of selected fruit and nuts.
2. Stir yogurt and juice concentrate until well blended.
3. Combine dressing with fruit mixture.
4. Serve on lettuce and garnish each serving with a slice of kiwi.

Serves 12

Fresh Fruit Salad
CAROLYN JONES

Salad Ingredients

1 fresh grapefruit, peeled and sectioned
2 oranges, peeled and sliced
1 pint fresh strawberries, cleaned
1 fresh melon (your choice), scooped into balls
  or cut into chunks
1 fresh pineapple, cut into bite-sized pieces
2 pears, peeled and sliced
2 apples, peeled and sliced
2 bananas, peeled and sliced

Dressing Ingredients

¼ cup fresh lemon juice
½ teaspoon ground ginger

Dash of mace
Dash of cardamom (extra, optional)
Whipped cream (optional)
Powdered sugar (optional)

Directions

1. Combine lemon juice, ginger, mace and cardamom.
2. Dip pear, apple and banana slices in lemon juice mixture.
3. Pour remaining lemon juice mixture over all.
4. Serve plain or with an additional dressing of whipped cream flavored with powdered sugar and cardamom.

Serves 6 to 8

Sweet and Sour Strawberry Fruit Salad
THETUS TENNEY

Ingredients

1 large carton fresh strawberries
1 large can pineapple slices, cut into bits
3 or 4 large bananas
1 small can toasted coconut
1 cup walnuts, sliced or broken
1 cup or small carton sour cream
2 heaping tablespoons brown sugar

Directions

1. Rinse and slice strawberries into mixing bowl.
2. Drain pineapple and add to strawberries, reserving juice in a separate bowl.
3. Slice bananas into pineapple juice to prevent them from turning dark.
4. Drain and discard pineapple juice; add bananas to strawberries and pineapple.
5. Add coconut and walnuts to fruit and mix well.
6. Pour sour cream into medium bowl. Add brown sugar and whip well. Pour dressing over fruit salad before serving.

Holiday Fruit Salad
THETUS TENNEY

Ingredients

1 can pitted, dark sweet cherries (extra cherries, optional)
1 can pineapple tidbits or chunks
3 large bananas
1 cup flaked coconut (extra, optional)
1 cup sliced pecans or almonds
1 8-ounce package cream cheese, softened
Coconut, flaked (optional)

Directions

1. Drain cherries, reserve juice, and rinse cherries with cold water.
2. Drain pineapple and reserve juice in a bowl (if chunks are used, cut into smaller pieces).
3. Slice bananas into bowl of pineapple juice to keep them from turning dark.
4. Drain and discard the pineapple juice. Combine cherries, pineapple, bananas, coconut and nuts and pour into a glass or crystal bowl.
5. Put cream cheese in medium bowl and separate into several pieces with a fork. Gradually add very small amounts of cherry juice to cheese and blend with an electric mixer. Add enough juice to make mixture thick but pourable.
6. Serve cheese dressing in a glass or crystal container (to best display dressing's beautiful color) beside fruit salad.
7. Garnish salad with a small mound of dressing, a cherry and a sprinkling of coconut, if desired.

Tabouli
SUZANNE HINN

Ingredients

¾ cup bulgur (wheat)
Water to cover bulgur
2 bunches fresh parsley
1 English cucumber, peeled and diced small
8 to 10 Roma tomatoes, diced small
1 or 2 green onions, diced
¼ cup extra virgin olive oil
Salt
¼ cup fresh mint, chopped
⅓ cup lemon juice
Romaine lettuce

Directions

1. Soak bulgur in water in a large mixing bowl. The water level should exceed the bulgur by a few inches. Set aside until bulgur no longer absorbs water, and drain well. Set aside.
2. Wash parsley well, drain and shake out the excess moisture. Remove stems and discard. Chop parsley very fine, using a food processor; add to bulgur.
3. Add cucumbers, tomatoes and onions and oil to wheat and parsley.
4. Season to taste with salt, mint and lemon juice. Pour over salad ingredient mixture.
5. Serve with Romaine lettuce leaves as a garnish. Tear leaves into large bite-size pieces and use to scoop up salad for eating.

Broccoli Salad
DIANE MODER

Salad Ingredients

2 large bunches fresh broccoli
4 ounces cheddar cheese, shredded
4 ounces mozzarella cheese, shredded
½ cup onion, finely chopped
1 pound bacon, cooked and crumbled

Dressing Ingredients

1 cup mayonnaise or salad dressing
2 teaspoons vinegar
½ cup sugar

Directions

1. Cut tops off broccoli and cut into small pieces. Mix with other salad ingredients.
2. Mix dressing ingredients together until sugar dissolves.
3. Pour over broccoli mixture. Chill for no more than 2 hours before serving.

Serves 10

Chinese Cabbage Salad
EVELYN STEELE

Salad Ingredients

1 head cabbage, shredded
1 green pepper
1 bunch green onions, chopped
4 tablespoons sesame seeds, toasted
1 cup slivered almonds, toasted
2 packages Top Ramen chicken or sesame flavor noodles, uncooked and crushed
Chicken, cooked and cut into chunks, or fruit such as pineapple or mandarin oranges (optional)

Dressing Ingredients

½ cup sugar
⅔ cup oil
½ cup rice vinegar (important)
2 Top Ramen flavor packets

Directions

1. Combine salad and dressing ingredients separately.
2. Mix dressing with salad just before serving.

Carolyn Sundseth's Variation: Add 1 cup shredded carrots to the chopped vegetables. Mix crushed Ramen noodles with ½ cup sunflower seeds and mix into salad just before serving.

Spinach Salad
VIRGINIA OTIS

Salad Ingredients

2 bunches fresh spinach
1 cup bean sprouts
6- to 8-ounce can water chestnuts, sliced
3 eggs, hard-boiled and diced
2 or 3 slices bacon, or equivalent amount bacon bits

Dressing Ingredients

½ cup sugar
½ cup ketchup
¼ cup vinegar
1 teaspoon salt

½ cup oil
1 teaspoon Worcestershire sauce
1 medium white onion, diced

Directions

1. Wash spinach, blot dry, and tear into pieces.
2. Combine spinach, bean sprouts, water chestnuts and eggs.
3. Fry bacon crisp, crumble, and set aside.
4. Combine all dressing ingredients in a jar with a lid and shake well.
5. Add bacon to the spinach mixture, toss with dressing, and serve.

Marinated Vegetable Salad
ANNA HAYFORD

Ingredients

1 1-pound can shoe-peg corn
1 1-pound can sliced green beans
1 1-pound can very small peas
1 cup celery, chopped
⅓ cup onion, minced
½ cup white vinegar
⅓ cup vegetable oil
¾ cup sugar
Salt
Freshly ground pepper

Directions

1. Drain all canned vegetables and place in a bowl; add celery and onion and mix together.
2. Heat and stir vinegar, vegetable oil and sugar until sugar is dissolved.
3. Add salt and pepper to taste.
4. Pour vinegar mixture over vegetables and refrigerate for 24 hours before serving.

Serves 8 to 10

Vegetable Salad and Creamy Herb Dressing
ANNA HAYFORD

Salad Ingredients

2 bunches radishes, thinly sliced
4 medium-sized cucumbers, pared, halved and thinly sliced
6 carrots, shredded
2 green peppers, seeded and diced
2 cups alfalfa sprouts

Creamy Herb Dressing

1 egg
1 small onion, quartered
1 clove garlic
2 teaspoons prepared mustard
½ teaspoon salt
¼ teaspoon pepper
1 teaspoon leaf tarragon
½ teaspoon leaf basil
¼ cup tarragon vinegar
1 cup vegetable oil
1 tablespoon parsley, minced

Directions

1. Refrigerate all salad ingredients separately until ready to serve.
2. Combine all ingredients for dressing, except oil and parsley, in the container of an electric blender.
3. Whirl 1 minute. With blender running, drizzle in vegetable oil very slowly until all oil is added and the dressing is thick and creamy.
4. Stir in parsley.
5. Pour dressing into a screw-top jar; refrigerate.
6. Just before serving, arrange vegetables in rows in salad bowls. Serve with dressing.

Makes 1¾ cups (serves 10)

Shrimp Oriental Salad
JANE HANSEN

Ingredients
1 1-pound can bean sprouts, rinsed and drained
2 cans shrimp, drained
¼ cup green onions, minced
¾ cup mayonnaise
1 tablespoon lemon juice
¼ cup celery, sliced
1 tablespoon soy sauce
1 can chow mein noodles
1 5-ounce can water chestnuts, drained and sliced
Lettuce

Directions
1. Combine all ingredients except noodles and water chestnuts. Let set in refrigerator overnight.
2. Before serving, add noodles and water chestnuts.
3. Serve on lettuce leaves.

Carrot Supreme
WANDA HANSEN

Ingredients
2 pounds carrots
1 slice white onion
1 green pepper, sliced
⅓ cup salad oil
⅔ cup sugar
1 can tomato soup
1 teaspoon mustard, dry or prepared
1 teaspoon Worcestershire sauce
½ teaspoon salt
1 teaspoon paprika
1 teaspoon pepper

Directions
1. Clean and slice the carrots diagonally; partially cook and cool.
2. Combine all other ingredients; pour over the carrots. Mix and put in the refrigerator until the next day.

Tip: The carrots may be served cold as a salad or reheated to serve as a side dish at dinner.

Vinaigrette Green Beans

This recipe was a gift from the Hitching Post in Austin, Texas.

VONETTE BRIGHT

Ingredients

3 tablespoons vinegar

½ cup olive oil

1 teaspoon salt

⅛ teaspoon freshly ground pepper

¼ teaspoon paprika

Dash cayenne pepper

1 tablespoon pimiento, finely chopped

1 tablespoon pickles, finely chopped

2 teaspoons finely chopped green pepper

1½ teaspoons parsley, finely chopped

1 teaspoon chives or onion, finely chopped

2 15-ounce cans green beans, drained

Directions

1. Slowly add vinegar and oil to salt, pepper, paprika and cayenne; beat thoroughly.
2. Add all vegetables except green beans to dressing.
3. Pour dressing over green beans; cook slowly over low heat until heated through.

Makes about 1 cup

Tip: Dressing may be made ahead and refrigerated.
Variation: Use dried pepper, parsley and onion instead of fresh ingredients.

Crab Spinach Soufflé

This is a party recipe for a special brunch or a bridal shower. It's easy to prepare and elegant to serve.

PATTI McGINNIS

Ingredients

1 package of Stouffer's frozen chopped spinach soufflé, defrosted

2 pounds small-curd cottage cheese

6 tablespoons flour

6 eggs

1 stick butter, diced

½ pound sharp cheddar cheese, diced

1 6- or 7½-ounce can crabmeat

Directions

1. Preheat oven to 350° F.
2. Mix all ingredients together and bake in a greased 9x13-inch pan for 1 hour.

Serves 10 to 12

Creamy Spinach
LADY BIRD JOHNSON

Ingredients

3 pounds fresh spinach or 2 10-ounce packages of
   frozen chopped spinach
6 tablespoons grated Parmesan cheese
6 tablespoons onion, finely minced
4 tablespoons instant dried onion
6 tablespoons heavy cream or half-and-half
4 tablespoons butter or margarine, melted
¼ teaspoon black pepper
A few grains of cayenne pepper
Salt to taste
½ cup cracker crumbs
1 tablespoon melted butter or margarine

Directions

1. Cook spinach until it wilts. Drain and chop coarsely.
2. Combine all ingredients except cracker crumbs and butter.
3. Pour mixture into a shallow buttered baking dish.
4. Sprinkle with cracker crumbs mixed with 1 tablespoon melted butter or margarine.
5. Bake in a moderately hot oven (375° F) 10 to 15 minutes or until golden and lightly crusted.

Serves 4 to 6

To increase recipe to serve 16 to 20:
8 10-ounce packages spinach
1⅓ cups Parmesan cheese
1 cup dried onion
1⅓ cups heavy cream
1 cup melted butter or margarine
2 cups cracker crumbs
¼ cup melted butter for crumbs

Rice Pilaf
KAY ARTHUR

Ingredients
¼ cup butter
1 cup uncooked rice
2 cups hot chicken broth
½ teaspoon salt
⅛ teaspoon pepper

Directions
1. Melt butter, add rice and stir-fry for 5 minutes.
2. Add broth and seasonings.
3. Cook covered for 18 to 20 minutes. Uncover and cook 5 minutes longer .

Suggestions: Thicken the broth with cornstarch, add mushrooms and serve in Pepperidge Farms patty shells (from the frozen-food section of your grocery). Serve with Chicken and Shrimp in Sour Cream Sauce (see index).

Sweet Potato Puff
DENISE FRANGIPANE

Ingredients
3 cups mashed sweet potatoes, unsweetened canned or fresh
¼ cup honey
¼ cup butter
2 eggs
⅓ cup milk
1 teaspoon vanilla
½ cup coconut, flaked or shredded
¼ cup date sugar, brown sugar or Sucanat
½ cup chopped pecans
2 tablespoons butter
¼ cup flour

Directions
1. Beat sweet potatoes until smooth. Add honey, ¼ cup butter, eggs, milk and vanilla.
2. Mix until fluffy. Stir in coconut.
3. Spoon into a greased 2½-quart baking dish.
4. Mix sugar, pecans, 2 tablespoons butter and flour until blended.
5. Sprinkle over sweet potatoes.
6. Bake uncovered at 350° F for 35 to 40 minutes.

Scalloped Pineapple

This is delicious with ham as a side dish.

ELAINE KEITH

Ingredients
7 slices bread, cubed into small pieces
1 stick margarine
1 large can crushed pineapple with juice
2 eggs, well beaten
1 cup sugar
3 tablespoons flour

Directions
1. Sauté bread cubes in margarine until soaked; do not brown.
2. Add pineapple with its juice, eggs, sugar and flour to the sautéed bread.
3. Pour mixture into a 2-quart casserole.
4. Bake at 350° F for 35 to 40 minutes.

Serves 10 to 12

Blue Lake String Beans

The flavor is improved if the ingredients are combined early in the morning, covered, stored and then baked just before serving.

ANNA HAYFORD

Ingredients
1 can string beans
2 tablespoons brown sugar
1 tablespoon vinegar
¼ cup almonds
1 can condensed cream of mushroom soup
½ cup sour cream
3 strips bacon, cut up and fried slowly
1 small onion, cut up

Directions
1. Drain juice from beans.
2. Blend all ingredients together and bake 30 to 45 minutes at 350° F.

Romaine Salad with Oranges, Bananas and Cashews

RHONNI GREIG

Salad Ingredients

2 heads of Romaine lettuce, washed (inner leaves make a crisper salad)

1 can mandarin oranges

2 medium bananas, sliced

1 cup cashews

Orange Poppy Seed Vinaigrette Dressing Ingredients

3 tablespoons sugar

1½ teaspoons orange peel, finely shredded

2 tablespoons orange juice that has been reduced from 1 cup by heating

2 tablespoons vinegar

1 tablespoon onion

Dash of pepper

⅓ cup salad oil (vegetable, corn or grape seed)

1 teaspoon poppy seeds

Directions

1. Combine all dressing ingredients except the salad oil and poppy seeds into a food processor bowl or blender container and process or blend until combined.
2. With the processor or blender running, slowly add salad oil in a steady stream through the hole or opening in the top.
3. Process or blend until mixture is thickened.
4. Stir in poppy seeds.
5. Cover and chill until needed. Shake before using.
6. Combine salad ingredients and toss with dressing just before serving.

We have found that a great thing to do when having children or teens over with their families is to have something they can get involved in. We have all the kids help in the kitchen to show that serving is fun and anyone can do it.

JEANNIE CEDAR

Ideas for Table Centerpieces

For a meal planned in the dining room, remember to make the centerpiece low enough for your guests to see each other and enjoy conversing. A centerpiece can extend down the center of the table for added effect.

You can use almost anything to create an interesting centerpiece. Consider using something old and charming, even whimsical, as a container for a floral centerpiece. Here are some other ideas that will add fun and interest to your table:

· An old-fashioned doll with a small basket beside her filled with a floral bouquet that looks like it was gathered from a field or meadow
· A stack of old books with an unusual candlestick placed on top and another candlestick (they don't have to match) beside the books (an old pair of reading glasses casually placed there for effect would also be interesting)
· A combination of various sizes and shapes of bottles—each filled with a few flowers and grouped together
· Ribbons, sparkling confetti, interesting twigs, fruits, vegetables, teddy bears, children's toys or shells arranged artfully
· An arrangement of individual little plants with a Scripture promise rolled up in scroll fashion (give each of the guests a plant as they leave)
· Knickknacks from around the house (seashells from your last beach trip might look elegant in a favorite crystal bowl or lattice cut-out dish).
· A lovely ivy plant or African violet moved from a kitchen window (dress up the pot with some fabric and ribbon and give it a new home in the center of your table).

Entrées

Javanese Dinner

Serve with tea; no salad or bread is needed. For dessert, serve Chinese cookies with pineapple sherbet or coconut ice cream. This recipe is a Campus Crusade family favorite from early ministry days. It's excellent for serving a crowd or for a shared meal with everyone bringing the ingredients.

VONETTE BRIGHT

Ingredients

5 stewing chickens
Water to cover chicken
Bouillon
Condensed cream of celery soup or cream of mushroom soup
Curry powder
Steamed rice for 40
1¼ gallons chow mein noodles (optional)
2 cups yellow onions, chopped
3 cups celery, chopped
5 cups Monterey Jack or cheddar cheese, grated
5 cups shredded coconut
5 cups crushed pineapple, drained
5 cups blanched almonds, cut into large pieces

Directions

1. Cover chicken with water and simmer until done. Bone and cut meat into chunks.
2. Make a clear gravy with the chicken broth by adding bouillon, soup and curry powder.
3. Put half of the gravy into a serving bowl and mix the other half with the chicken pieces.

Set out ingredients on a buffet table and have guests help themselves to these approximate amounts, in the order given:

1 large serving of rice, patted down
2 tablespoons chicken in gravy
1 heaping tablespoon chow mein noodles, if desired
1 tablespoon onion
1 tablespoon celery
2 tablespoons cheese
2 tablespoons coconut
2 tablespoons pineapple
2 tablespoons almonds
Chicken gravy to cover

Serves 40

Roasted Beef Brisket

This brisket recipe is so simple. It is a wonderful idea for Christmas holiday entertaining because it is made ahead of time, the day before you plan to serve it.

JANE HANSEN

Ingredients
1 7-pound beef brisket
1 package dry onion soup mix
1 medium onion, sliced
2 stalks celery, chopped
1 12-ounce bottle chili sauce
½ cup water
1½ cups club soda

Directions
1. Brown the meat in a skillet.
2. Place meat in ovenproof pan with lid, sprinkle with dry onion soup mix and top with onion slices and celery.
3. Pour chili sauce over meat.
4. Pour water into chili sauce jar, rinse jar and pour water over brisket.
5. Cover and bake at 350° F for 45 minutes per pound.
6. One hour before meat is finished cooking, add club soda.
7. Cool and thinly slice meat.
8. Refrigerate overnight.
9. Reheat for 30 minutes in sauce before serving.

Serves 10

Suggestion: Serve with cooked peas with mint sauce, a good side dish with the beef brisket. Cook the amount of peas you desire, and then just before serving, drain the water and add mint sauce or jelly to taste.

Home from work late with no time for marinating meat? Pound meat lightly with a mallet, pierce with a fork, sprinkle lightly with meat tenderizer and add marinade. Refrigerate in a plastic bag for about 20 minutes. You will have succulent, tender meat.

DIANE MODER

Beef Tenderloin à la Bradshaw
MARY LANCE SISK

Ingredients

1 beef tenderloin
Garlic salt
6 tablespoons (¾ stick) butter
¼ cup soy sauce
Lemon pepper
1 cup Burgundy wine

Directions

1. Salt tenderloin with garlic salt and sear in oven at 425° F for 10 minutes.
2. Heat together butter, soy sauce and lemon pepper until butter has melted. Add wine and mix well.
3. As soon as the tenderloin has been seared, pour wine mixture over it. Cook at about 350° F, basting every 10 minutes until beef is done. The time on this varies from 20 to 30 minutes according to the size and piece of meat.

Suggestion: Sometimes I marinate the tenderloin in the mixture for about 3 hours before baking it. If it's a large piece of meat, you may want to double the marinade recipe.

Hawaiian Beef Sticks
VIRGINIA OTIS

Ingredients

2-inch piece of fresh ginger, sliced
2 cloves garlic, mashed
2 small onions, chopped
1 cup soy sauce
4 tablespoons sugar
8 small dried hot chili peppers
2 tablespoons red wine vinegar
4 teaspoons cornstarch
½ cup water
2 pounds beef sirloin

Directions

1. In small pan, combine fresh ginger, garlic, onions, soy sauce, sugar, chili peppers and vinegar. Cook over medium heat until slightly thick, about 20 minutes.
2. Combine the cornstarch with water. Gradually stir cornstarch into sauce and cook, stirring until clear and thickened.
3. Pour mixture through a wire strainer, pressing out all juices, and discard the pulp; cool.
4. Cut beef into bite-sized pieces; add to marinade and allow to stand covered for 2 hours.
5. Thread 2 to 3 pieces of meat on each skewer; barbecue over hot coals or broil.

Makes 48

Shepherd's Pie
DORIS BUSH

Ingredients

1 pound lean ground beef
1 onion, chopped
1 clove garlic, minced
1 large can stewed tomatoes
Salt
Pepper
2 cups mashed potatoes, fresh or instant
Parmesan cheese

Optional Ingredients

Raisins
Cut corn
Sweet peas
Cut green beans
½ cup red cooking wine
Parmesan cheese

Directions

1. Brown ground beef in skillet and drain off fat.
2. Push meat to the side of the pan and fry onion and garlic.
3. When onion and garlic are lightly brown, stir in the browned ground beef.
4. Add canned tomatoes.
5. Season with salt and pepper.
6. Stir in your choice of optional ingredients.
7. Transfer the mixture to a baking dish and top with mashed potatoes and Parmesan cheese.
8. Bake at 325° F for 1 hour.

Serves 4

Suggestion: Serve hot with French bread.

During the holidays I have put a few fresh pinecones on a piece of foil and placed them in a warm oven (around 200° F) for about 10 minutes. I then open the oven door and the house is filled with a fresh pine aroma.

SANDRA WEZOWICZ

Hamburgers Hawaiian

This is a dish I used a lot when we first entered the ministry and were on a tight budget.
I served it over rice, with a salad, hot rolls and a nice dessert.

ANNA HAYFORD

Hamburger Ingredients

⅔ cup evaporated milk
1½ pounds ground beef
½ cup onion, chopped
⅔ cup cracker crumbs
1 teaspoon seasoning salt
Fat for frying

Sweet and Sour Sauce Ingredients

1 13½-ounce can pineapple chunks
1 cup pineapple juice (add water to juice to make one cup)
2 tablespoons cornstarch
¼ cup vinegar (or less to taste)
¼ cup brown sugar
2 tablespoons soy sauce
1 cup green pepper, coarsely chopped

Directions

1. Combine milk, ground beef, onion, cracker crumbs and salt.
2. Form six 4-inch individual patties by pressing each one between pieces of waxed paper.
3. Brown patties in a skillet with a small amount of fat.
4. Pour off fat as the patties begin to brown.
5. Drain pineapple and mix pineapple juice with cornstarch, vinegar, brown sugar and soy sauce.
6. Heat in saucepan to thicken.
7. Add pineapple chunks and green pepper.
8. Cover hamburgers with sauce.
9. Simmer over low heat 15 minutes or until heated through.

Zucchini Lasagna

Zucchini slices are substituted for noodles. It's excellent!

WANDA HANSEN

Ingredients

1 pound ground beef
1 medium onion
2 cups tomato sauce
1 clove garlic, minced
1 teaspoon sweet basil
½ teaspoon oregano
12 ounces dry cottage cheese or ricotta cheese
½ cup grated Romano or Parmesan cheese, divided
2 eggs, beaten
Butter
1½ pounds zucchini, cut lengthwise into ¼″ slices
3 tablespoons flour
½ cup shredded mozzarella cheese

Directions

1. Preheat oven to 350° F.
2. Brown ground beef and onion; drain off fat and set aside.
3. Combine tomato sauce, garlic, basil and oregano in a saucepan; simmer for 10 minutes and then add the browned ground beef.
4. Mix together the cottage cheese, Romano cheese and eggs.
5. Butter a 9-inch square pan and layer in two layers of zucchini sprinkled lightly with flour, ½ the cheese mixture and half the meat mixture.
6. Top the first layer with ½ cup shredded mozzarella cheese.
7. Top the second layer with ¼ cup Romano cheese.
8. Bake uncovered for 45 minutes at 350° F.
9. Remove from the oven and let stand 20 minutes before serving.

My favorite centerpiece is a wicker basket lined with foil and containing three pillar candles centered in the basket to complement the season or the color scheme. Fill the basket around the candles with potpourri and let it spill over; you can even scatter potpourri to make the table look festive. Trim the basket with ribbon of a complementary color. The smell is delightful! It's easy, inexpensive and casual; and the candles bring a warm glow. In the summer I take old bottles of different shapes and sizes, fill them with fresh flowers and tie two or three bottles together with pieces of ribbon or raffia.

JOANNE MECKSTROTH

Barbecue Beef Marinade
CECI SHEETS

Ingredients

3 to 4 pounds beef roast, 3 inches thick
2 tablespoons ketchup
1½ teaspoons unflavored meat tenderizer
1 tablespoon soy sauce
2 cloves of garlic or equivalent amount of garlic powder
6 tablespoons wine vinegar or 4 tablespoons cider vinegar
  (do not use white vinegar)
2 tablespoons oil
1 tablespoon prepared mustard

Directions

1. Place meat in a shallow dish; mix all ingredients together and pour over meat.
2. Refrigerate for 36 to 48 hours, turning occasionally.
3. Barbecue on outside grill or broil in oven. Place meat 3 inches from the heat; barbecue or broil 10 minutes on each side.
4. Reduce heat, or if grilling, raise grill. Continue to cook 20 minutes for medium, or longer for well-done meat.

Serves 5

Cabbage Rolls
These can be prepared ahead of time and are even good the next day.
CAROL TORRANCE

Ingredients

1 cup rice, cooked
Water for rice and cabbage
1½ pounds extra-lean ground beef
1 teaspoon salt
1 teaspoon pepper
½ teaspoon garlic salt
1 large onion, chopped
4 tablespoons evaporated milk
1 egg
1 8- to 10-ounce can tomatoes, drained and diced; reserve juice
2 large cans tomato sauce, divided
1 large head cabbage

Directions

1. Spray a 9x12-inch baking pan with Pam cooking spray.
2. Cook rice and mix with uncooked ground beef, salt, pepper, garlic salt, onion, milk, egg, tomatoes, and ½ can of tomato sauce.
3. Carefully remove leaves from head of cabbage and drop leaves, a few at a time, into boiling water. Cook until tender; drain on paper towels.
4. Scoop a generous spoonful of the meat mixture onto each cabbage leaf and roll to enclose filling. Place in a prepared pan.
5. Cover cabbage rolls with remaining tomato sauce and juice from tomatoes.
6. Cover with foil or a lid and cook one hour at 350° F and check for doneness.

Stuffed Chicken Breasts with Mushroom Sauce
RHONNI GREIG

Chicken Ingredients

6 chicken breasts, boned and skinned (remove the skin
to cut down fat)
Optional:
  1 package seasoned bread stuffing
  1 cup apple juice
  Celery, chopped
Seasoned flour
Butter, melted
Paprika

Homemade Stuffing Ingredients

7 slices bread, torn in small pieces
½ cup apple juice
¼ teaspoon paprika
1 teaspoon poultry seasoning
3 tablespoons butter, melted
½ teaspoon salt
¼ teaspoon pepper
1 medium apple, pared, cored and chopped

Directions

1. If packaged stuffing is used: Prepare stuffing according to
   the directions on the package, but use apple juice for the
   liquid, and celery instead of onion.
2. If homemade stuffing is desired: Combine all ingredients
   in a bowl.

3. Flatten chicken breasts and place a good portion of stuffing
   in the middle of the each chicken breast.
4. Wrap chicken around the stuffing and secure with two
   wooden sticks.
5. Sprinkle with seasoned flour and coat with melted butter.
6. Place on flat baking sheet. Sprinkle with paprika and bake
   at 350° F for 1 hour.

Tip: This can be made the night before and stored in the refrigerator, but it will require more time to bake.

Mushroom Sauce Ingredients

½ pound fresh mushrooms, sliced
¾ cup onions, chopped
Butter or margarine
1 can condensed cream of mushroom soup
1 small carton sour cream

Directions

1. Sauté onions and mushrooms in butter or margarine; put in
   double boiler and add mushroom soup.
2. Add sour cream at the last minute and heat, being careful
   not to boil.

Note: The sauce can be made early in the day, but add the sour
cream at the last minute.

Chicken-Broccoli Casserole
DIANE MODER

Ingredients

3 packages frozen whole or chopped broccoli,
  or use fresh, cooked
6 chicken breasts, cooked
2 cans condensed cream of chicken soup
1 cup mayonnaise
2 teaspoons lemon juice
3 teaspoons cooking sherry (optional)
¾ cup sharp cheddar cheese, shredded

Directions

1. Arrange cooked broccoli in a 9x13-inch pan or large flat casserole dish.
2. Cut chicken into large bite-sized pieces and place over broccoli.
3. Mix together soup, mayonnaise, lemon juice and sherry (if desired) and pour over broccoli and chicken.
4. Bake covered for 45 minutes; then remove from oven and sprinkle cheese on top.
5. Cover again and bake another 15 minutes, or until bubbly and very hot.

Serves 6 to 8

Chicken Mandalay
ZEE JONES

Ingredients

4 chicken breasts
2 tablespoons curry powder
2 or 3 tablespoons flour
1 teaspoon salt
Dash of pepper
1 tablespoon shortening
2 beef bouillon cubes
1 cup water
1 large onion, chopped
1 tablespoon soy sauce
1 tablespoon Worcestershire sauce
1 tablespoon sugar
1 can apricots

Directions

1. Remove skin from chicken and shake chicken pieces in bag with curry powder, flour, salt and pepper.
2. Brown chicken in shortening.
3. Dissolve beef bouillon cubes in hot water.
4. Remove browned chicken from pan and place in large casserole dish.
5. Place bouillon mixture, onion, soy sauce and Worcestershire sauce, sugar and apricots in the pan used to brown chicken. Bring mixture to a boil; then pour it over chicken in casserole dish, cover and bake at 325° F for 2 hours.

Fluffy Rice and Chicken
NANCY McGUIRK

Ingredients

1 can condensed cream of mushroom soup
1 soup can of milk
¾ cup uncooked regular rice
1 4-ounce can mushroom stems and pieces, undrained
1 envelope onion soup mix
4 to 6 pieces of chicken

Directions

1. Heat oven to 350° F.
2. Mix mushroom soup and milk; reserve ½ cup of the mixture.
3. Mix remaining soup mixture, rice, mushrooms (with liquid) and half the onion soup mix.
4. Pour into ungreased 8x11½-inch baking dish; place chicken on top.
5. Pour reserved soup mixture over chicken; sprinkle with remaining onion soup mix.
6. Cover with foil and bake 1 hour. Uncover and bake 15 minutes longer.

Serves 4 to 5

Poppy Seed Chicken
BARBARA JAMES

Ingredients

4 to 6 boneless chicken breasts or a 3-pound chicken
Water to cover chicken
1 cup sour cream
1 can condensed cream of chicken soup
1 cup chicken broth
1 tablespoon lemon juice
2 teaspoons poppy seeds
6 tablespoon butter, melted
2 cups Ritz Crackers, crushed

Directions

1. Boil chicken in water until done and remove from broth.
2. Drain and cut chicken into small pieces.
3. Mix chopped chicken with remaining ingredients except butter and crackers.
4. Place chicken mixture in a casserole dish.
5. Mix melted butter with crushed crackers and stir until moistened.
6. Top chicken with crushed buttered crackers. (Dot with additional butter, if desired.)
7. Bake in moderate oven (350° F) until brown, approximately 30 to 40 minutes.

Chicken and Shrimp in Sour Cream Sauce

KAY ARTHUR

Ingredients

3 tablespoons butter
3 tablespoons flour
1 cup chicken broth
½ teaspoon garlic salt
⅛ teaspoon white pepper
Pinch of nutmeg
½ to 1 cup sour cream
1½ cups shrimp, cooked and diced
1½ cups chicken, cooked and diced

Directions

1. Melt butter in a saucepan, stir in flour, and cook until bubbly. Slowly add chicken broth and cook until thickened.
2. Season sauce with garlic salt, pepper and nutmeg; then stir in sour cream.
3. Add shrimp and chicken, and heat but do not boil.

Suggestion: Serve over Rice Pilaf (see index).

Chicken Pot Pie

CECI SHEETS

Ingredients

1 chicken, cooked, deboned and diced
1 can condensed cream of chicken soup
½ can water
1 medium onion
½ can green peas, drained
3 potatoes, partially cooked and diced
3 carrots, partially cooked and diced
1½ cups self-raising flour
1½ cups buttermilk
6 tablespoons margarine, melted
2½ cups chicken broth

Directions

1. Place chicken in the bottom of a deep roasting pan.
2. Mix soup and water and pour over chicken.
3. Add onion, peas, potatoes and carrots.
4. Mix flour, buttermilk and margarine in a separate bowl and pour over vegetables.
5. Pour broth over all.
6. Bake uncovered for 1½ hours at 350° F.

Note: Be sure that the top is lightly brown. Let stand for 10 minutes before serving.

Viva El Pollo
CECI SHEETS

Ingredients

1 whole chicken
Water to cover chicken
10 flour tortillas
1 can condensed cream of chicken soup
1 can condensed cream of mushroom soup
½ cup milk
1 medium onion, grated
2 cans diced green chilies
5 tablespoons chicken broth, divided
1 pound cheddar cheese, grated

Note: This recipe must be prepared 24 hours before you serve it.

Directions

1. Boil chicken until done; allow to cool and then debone and cut into large pieces.
2. Cut tortillas into 1-inch squares (stack and cut them all at once with a sharp knife).
3. Mix soups, milk, onion and chilies.
4. Grease a large, shallow baking dish.
5. Place 2 tablespoons of chicken broth in the bottom of the dish.
6. Add about 3 tablespoons of broth to the soup mixture.
7. Layer tortillas, chicken pieces and soup mixture, ending with soup mixture.
8. Cover and refrigerate 24 hours.
9. Before baking, top with cheese and bake uncovered at 325° F for 1½ hours.

Chicken Casserole
MARILYN TUCKER QUAYLE

Ingredients

1 whole chicken, cooked, deboned and cut into bite-sized pieces
½ cup slivered almonds
1 cup celery, finely chopped
1½ cup onion, finely chopped
2 cans condensed cream of chicken soup
2 cans water chestnuts, drained and sliced
1½ teaspoon tarragon
12 ounces medium sharp cheddar cheese, grated
1½ cups potato chips, crushed

Directions

1. Preheat oven to 450° F.
2. Mix all the above ingredients, except cheese and chips, and spread evenly in a 9x13-inch casserole dish.
3. Top with the cheese and chips.
4. Place in a preheated 450°F oven and immediately turn oven down to 350° F.
5. Bake for 30 minutes and watch closely. Do not allow to bubble or the sauce will separate.

Baked Barbecued Spareribs

This recipe works well to serve a large crowd, as it can be done well in advance and warmed up at the last minute.

GRETCHEN FINCH MAHONEY

Ingredients

3 cups water
1½ cups ketchup
1½ cups brown sugar
½ tablespoon Worcestershire sauce
1 teaspoon salt
1 teaspoon chili powder
4 drops Tabasco sauce
4 pounds farmer, or country style, pork spareribs
1½ large lemons, thinly sliced
1 large yellow onion, thinly sliced

Directions

1. Combine first seven ingredients in a saucepan and bring to a boil. Reduce heat and simmer for at least 30 minutes.
2. Remove all large chunks of fat from ribs. Place ribs in a flat baking pan or roaster.
3. Cover with lemon and onion slices. Cover tightly with lid or aluminum foil and bake at 325° F for 2 hours or until well done.
4. Pour off and discard all fat.
5. Baste with some of the sauce and continue baking, uncovered, at 400° F. Baste with additional sauce as needed to keep moist.

Suggestion: These are great served with corn on the cob, French bread and Poppy Seed Citrus Salad (see index).

Chalupa

CINDY JACOBS

Ingredients

3 to 4 pounds pork loin roast
1 pound pinto beans
2 cloves garlic, chopped
2 tablespoons chili powder
1 tablespoon ground cumin
1 teaspoon oregano
1 small can long green chilies, drained
1 tablespoon salt

Directions

1. Put all ingredients in a large pan and cover with water. Cover and cook over low heat. Add water if needed.
2. After 6 hours, take out bones and break up roast with fork. Cook uncovered until mixture thickens, about 1 hour.

Suggestion: Serve in small bowls over a bed of crisp corn chips, an English muffin or in a tostado shell and add any or all of the following: shredded lettuce, hot sauce, diced tomatoes and avocados, ripe olives, grated longhorn or Jack cheese, chopped onions.

Spaghetti Pie

I often give this recipe away with Proverbs 21:9, which says it's better to live in the corner of an attic than with a crabby woman in a lovely home, as a reminder that we have a choice and that our attitude sets the tone of our home.

KATHY TROCCOLI

Ingredients
1 pound spaghetti
6 eggs
¾ cup grated Parmesan or Romano cheese
1 teaspoon salt
Olive oil
8 ounces mozzarella cheese, sliced or shredded

Suggestion: This is great with a salad and some crispy Italian bread!

Directions
1. Boil spaghetti until tender and drain.
2. Beat eggs, cheese and salt together.
3. Coat spaghetti with egg mixture.
4. Coat round skillet with olive oil.
5. Place ½ of the cooked spaghetti in the skillet.
6. Place one layer of mozzarella cheese on top of spaghetti.
7. Top the cheese with the rest of the spaghetti noodles.
8. Cook over low heat until golden brown.
9. Cover with a plate, flip and return to pan, so other side can be heated. Heat until golden brown.

Summer Spaghetti Sauce

In this dish, the contact of the very cold sauce with the hot spaghetti releases a unique and delicious flavor. The resulting tepid pasta salad makes a refreshing lunch or light supper for a hot summer day.

PATTI MCGINNIS

Ingredients
1 pound firm, ripe fresh plum tomatoes, finely chopped
1 medium onion or scallions, finely chopped
6 pitted green olives, chopped
2 medium cloves garlic, pressed
⅓ cup fresh parsley, chopped

Directions
1. Combine all ingredients, cover and refrigerate until ready to use.

Serves 4 to 6

Suggestion: This versatile sauce may also be served as a relish with grilled meats, as a dressing for mixed greens or stirred into cooled cooked rice or risotto.

Alaskan Quiche
JoAnne Meckstroth

Ingredients

1 frozen 9" deep-dish pie shell or make your
   favorite pie crust recipe
1 4- to 6-ounce can smoked salmon
1 cup Monterey Jack cheese, shredded
4 eggs
½ teaspoon salt
¾ teaspoon sugar
2 cups whipping cream
⅓ cup onions, chopped
Cheddar cheese, shredded
Cayenne pepper

Directions

1. Defrost pie shell but do not bake.
2. Arrange smoked salmon in unbaked pie shell.
3. Top salmon with Monterey Jack cheese.
4. Beat together eggs, salt, sugar and whipping cream.
5. Mix onions into egg mixture.
6. Pour egg mixture over cheese and salmon in pie shell and sprinkle with cheddar cheese and cayenne pepper.
7. Bake at 450° F for 15 minutes; then reduce temperature to 300° F and continue to bake for 30 minutes.

Serves 5 to 6

Crustless Tuna Quiche
Jean Vandenbos

Ingredients

1 tablespoon butter
⅓ cup green onion, sliced
¼ cup chopped red or green pepper
4 eggs
3 tablespoons flour
¼ teaspoon salt
¼ teaspoon dry mustard
⅛ teaspoon pepper
1½ cups skim milk
1½ cups (6 ounces) cheddar cheese, grated
1 6½-ounce can tuna in water, drained and flaked
1 tomato, cut into six wedges

Directions

1. Preheat oven to 350° F.
2. Melt butter in small skillet.
3. Sauté onion and pepper until tender, about 3 minutes.
4. Combine eggs, flour and seasonings in a medium-sized mixing bowl and beat until well blended.
5. Stir in milk and add cheese, tuna and sautéed vegetables; mix well.
6. Pour into well-buttered 9-inch pie plate.
7. Bake 45 to 50 minutes or until knife inserted near center comes out clean.
8. Let cool 10 minutes before serving.
9. Garnish each serving with a tomato wedge.

Serves 6

Fabulous Fiesta Frittata Olé
ESTHER ILNISKY

Ingredients

10 large eggs

Salt

Pepper

2 tablespoons water, milk or cream

½ cup sausage, bacon, ham or other meat, cooked and crumbled

½ cup tomato, chopped

Butter or cooking spray

½ cup onion, chopped

½ cup red or green pepper, diced

½ cup mushrooms, sliced

½ to ¾ cup extra sharp cheddar cheese, shredded

Parsley and assorted vegetables or tomato rosettes and lettuce

Directions

1. Break eggs into medium-sized mixing bowl and whisk until well blended.
2. Whisk salt, pepper and water, milk or cream into eggs.
3. Add cooked meat(s) and tomato.
4. Heat a skillet over medium heat and melt butter or coat with cooking spray.
5. Sauté onions, pepper and mushrooms, cooking slowly until soft.
6. Pour egg mixture evenly over the mushroom mixture.
7. As egg mixture begins to set, gently lift edges of frittata and coax remaining egg mixture under edges to cook more quickly and evenly. Be careful not to overcook or cook too quickly! You will need to repeat this step more than once. Heat may need to be reduced to ensure egg mixture cooks without getting tough. Just before frittata is ready, sprinkle top with cheese and cover skillet to encourage cheese to melt.
8. Remove frittata from skillet with broad, flat spatula to serving plate. Garnish with curly parsley and assorted vegetables or a simple tomato rosette resting on a lettuce leaf in the middle of your golden frittata.

Suggestion: Be creative and make it colorful! Actually any bits and pieces of leftover meats or veggies can be added to this dish. You could also do it strictly vegetarian and/or add sliced or diced cooked potatoes.

Serving Ideas: Add some tea and coffee, fresh fruit, small croissants and your best homemade sweet bread with butter and jam. A side dish of salsa or picanté sauce makes a great topping for the frittata and adds a Latin flavor to your gathering.

Egg Soufflé
A make-ahead delight!

Carolyn Jones

Ingredients

15 slices white bread (preferably day-old)
½ pound cheddar cheese, grated
2 teaspoons onion flakes
6 eggs
4 cups milk
½ teaspoon salt
⅓ cup butter
⅔ cup slivered almonds

Directions

1. Remove the crust from the bread and cube.
2. Mix bread cubes, cheese and onion flakes and arrange in a buttered 9x13-inch baking dish.
3. Beat together eggs, milk and salt; pour over bread mixture.
4. Melt butter and drizzle over the top.
5. Sprinkle top with almonds.
6. Cover and refrigerate over night.
7. Bake at 350° F for one hour.
8. Serve immediately, as it deflates as it stands.

Serves 10 to 12

It's a wonderful concept to have your house presentable at all times, but it's not always possible. Choose a room that you will always keep picked up. Maybe you have a living room that can be off-limits to food, drink and TV. Also, keep the nearest bathroom clean, with a clean hand towel nearby, so it can be interchanged quickly. One of my favorite household tools is a Fuller Brush push broom. It picks up things on the carpet quickly and leaves those "I just vacuumed my carpet" marks on the floor. If the kids tend to leave things in the living areas of your home, keep a basket on the stairs or near the hallway to hold the things that have been left about.

Ceci Sheets

Quickie Little Pizzas
JEANNIE CEDAR

Ingredients

English muffins, hoagie buns, French bread or other
   bread product (be creative!)
1 jar Ragu Spaghetti Sauce (or pizza sauce)
Pepperoni, browned ground beef or any other meat
Mozzarella, cheddar and/or Monterey Jack cheese, grated
Black olives
Parmesan cheese, grated
Tomatoes, sliced or diced

Directions

1. Cut your bread choice in half.
2. Spread with spaghetti sauce.
3. Spread with choice of meat and grated cheese.
4. Top with olives, Parmesan cheese and tomatoes.
5. Broil for a few minutes, watching closely.

Festive Touches

Have plenty of candles around your dining area and don't limit them just to your table. Candlelight always adds a special ambience and glow to your room as well as to your guests.

Don't be afraid to mix your dishes and silverware. It's more pleasing to the eye if the colors are coordinated, but it is perfectly acceptable to blend the things you have.

For holiday parties:

- If using stemware during the Christmas season, tie a sprig of holly to the base of each guest's water glass. Wired ribbon also makes a beautifully formed bow.
- For Valentine's Day, place a carnation at each place setting.
- For Easter, consider placing a miniature basket at each setting. Fill each basket with shredded paper and tiny chocolate eggs, or nestle in the paper homemade frosted sugar cookies cut out in the shape of carrots. This little gift doubles as your place card when you put the name of each guest on a small piece of parchment paper and tie it to the basket handle with pastel-colored ribbon.
- For summertime get-togethers, consider using fresh fruit to dress up the table and help your guests find their places. Using yarn or string, attach a guest's name to the stem of a delicious apple or pear.
- For Thanksgiving, consider using brightly colored fall leaves underneath unlit scented votives.
- For birthday parties, greet gift givers with presents for *them:* small wrapped boxes containing a votive candle, homemade goodies or tiny picture frames.

Desserts

Citrus Cake
ESTHER ILNISKY

Cake Ingredients
1 package yellow cake mix
½ cup vegetable oil
3 large eggs
1 11-ounce can mandarin orange slices, including liquid

Directions
1. Grease and lightly flour two 8- or 9-inch round cake pans.
2. Blend together all cake ingredients in mixing bowl with electric beater for 30 seconds at slow speed and then for 2 minutes at medium speed.
3. Divide batter evenly into two prepared cake pans.
4. Bake in preheated oven at 350° F for approximately 28 to 32 minutes.
5. Test with cake tester for doneness.
6. Remove from oven and cool on a rack for 10 minutes.
7. Remove cake from pan, cover and cool completely.

Icing Ingredients
1 large container Cool Whip
1 small package vanilla Jell-O Instant Pudding
1 large can crushed pineapple, including liquid

Directions
1. Mix Cool Whip, instant pudding and entire contents of can of crushed pineapple together until well blended. Set aside in refrigerator.
2. With a thin sharp knife, slice each cake layer into two layers, resulting in four cake layers.
3. Place first layer on serving plate and spread with approximately ¼ of the icing mixture. Repeat with each of the next two layers.
4. Place last layer of cake on top and finish with the remaining frosting. You needn't be too precise; this cake looks even more delectable with the icing peeking out and spilling down the sides a bit.
5. Garnish as desired. (Reserve a few orange slices and place them with some greens on top; then add a little coconut to the top or to each layer, if you really love coconut; and/or arrange some lemon leaves around the base of the cake.)

Best Banana Cake
DEE JEPSEN

Cake Ingredients

½ cup margarine
2 cups sugar
3 ripe bananas, mashed
3 eggs
2 cups flour
1 teaspoon baking soda
2 teaspoons baking powder
½ teaspoon salt
1 cup buttermilk (or sour a cup of milk with
   a tablespoon of vinegar)
2 teaspoons vanilla
1 cup walnuts, chopped

Directions

1. Cream the margarine and sugar.
2. Beat in bananas and eggs.
3. Mix together flour, baking soda, baking powder and salt.
4. Add dry mixture to original mixture, alternating the dry mixture and buttermilk.
5. Beat in vanilla and add nuts.
6. Pour into 9x13x2-inch pan or two 9-inch round pans.
7. Bake at 350° F for 35 to 40 minutes.

Frosting Ingredients

8 ounces cream cheese, softened
½ cup margarine
Pinch of salt
1 pound confectioners' sugar
1 cup walnuts, chopped

Directions

1. Mix all ingredients except nuts together until creamy. Spread over slightly warm cake and sprinkle with chopped nuts.

Peach Melba
JOANNE MECKSTROTH

Ingredients

Canned peach halves (allow one peach for each serving)
Raspberry sauce
Vanilla ice cream
Butter cookies

Directions

1. Place 1 peach half, cut side up, in each dessert dish.
2. Fill peach cavity with raspberry sauce.
3. Top with a scoop of vanilla ice cream.
4. Drizzle raspberry sauce on top.

Suggestion: Serve in footed, stemmed or small individual dessert bowls, or custard cups; and serve with butter cookies.

Best Carrot Cake

A mixer is not needed for this cake batter.

DEE JEPSEN

Cake Ingredients

3 cups carrots, grated
1½ cups oil
2 cups flour
2 teaspoons baking soda
1 teaspoon salt
2 teaspoons cinnamon
2 cups sugar
4 eggs
1 teaspoon vanilla
1 cup walnut pieces

Directions

1. Preheat oven to 350° F.
2. Pour the oil over carrots.
3. Mix together flour, baking soda, salt, cinnamon and sugar.
4. Add one egg at a time to dry mixture, beating after each egg is added.
5. Add vanilla.
6. Add carrot and oil mixture to the above batter, using a wooden spoon or other similar utensil.
7. Add the walnut pieces and mix.
8. Bake in 3 greased and floured 8- or 9-inch layer pans, or a large flat cake pan (at least a 9x13-inch pan), in preheated 350° F oven (or slightly less) for 45 minutes (test!).

Frosting Ingredients

8 ounces cream cheese
⅔ stick butter or margarine
1 teaspoon vanilla
Pinch of salt
1 pound confectioners' sugar
1 cup of walnut pieces

Directions

1. Cream first five ingredients together, frost cooled cake, and sprinkle with walnut pieces to decorate.

Apricot Nectar Cake
This is my favorite for Thanksgiving.
CECI SHEETS

Cake Ingredients
1/4 teaspoon cream of tartar
4 small eggs, separated
2 tablespoons sugar
1 lemon supreme or white cake mix (Duncan Hines works well)
1/4 teaspoon pure lemon extract
2/3 cup oil
3/4 cup apricot nectar

Directions
1. Add cream of tartar to egg whites and beat until stiff.
2. Beat in sugar.
3. In separate bowl, beat together the remaining ingredients until well mixed.
4. Fold in egg whites.
5. Bake in a tube pan for 30 to 45 minutes at 325° F.

Icing Ingredients
1 cup apricot nectar
1 cup sugar
2 tablespoons lemon juice

Directions
1. Combine all ingredients in a pot and bring to a boil; boil for 5 minutes.
2. Pour over warm cake.

Quick Peach Cobbler
CECI SHEETS

Ingredients
1 cup sugar
1 cup milk
1 cup self-rising flour (must be self-rising)
1 stick of margarine, melted
1 large can of cling peaches, drained

Directions
1. Mix together sugar, milk, flour and margarine and pour into a 2-quart baking dish.
2. Cut the peaches into 1-inch pieces and place on top. Bake uncovered about 30 to 40 minutes at 350 to 375° F or until crust is brown.

Serves 4

Piña Colada Cake

This recipe is from my mother, Margaret Zachary.

VONETTE BRIGHT

Ingredients

1 Duncan Hines extra-rich yellow cake mix
1 can sweetened condensed milk
1 cup nonalcoholic piña colada mix
1 8-ounce carton Cool Whip
1 small can flaked coconut

Directions

1. Bake the cake mix according to the package directions.
2. Immediately after removing from the oven, pierce the cake thoroughly with a toothpick.
3. Pour the condensed milk evenly over the top; let the cake cool.
4. Pour the piña colada mix over the cake and allow time for the mix to be absorbed.
5. Refrigerate, if desired.
6. Spread Cool Whip on top and sprinkle with coconut before serving.

Favorite Fruitcake

BARBARA JAMES

Ingredients

1½ cups butter, softened
2 cups sugar
6 eggs
4 cups sifted all-purpose flour
2 teaspoons baking powder
½ teaspoon salt
½ cup fresh orange juice
1½ cups chopped pecans
1 pound candied fruit
1 7-ounce can flaked coconut
¼ cup all-purpose flour

Directions

1. Preheat oven to 225° F.
2. Line bottom of tube pan with wax paper.
3. Cream butter and sugar.
4. Add eggs one at a time, beating after each addition.
5. Sift flour with baking powder and salt.
6. Add flour mixture to creamed mixture alternately with orange juice.
7. Mix pecans, candied fruit and coconut with ¼ cup flour; fold into batter.
8. Spoon batter into pan.
9. Bake 4 hours (start checking for doneness at 3½ hours).
10. Cool 2 hours in the pan.

Cindy's Awesome Cake
CINDY JACOBS

Cake Ingredients

2 cups flour
2/3 teaspoon salt
1 1/3 cups sugar
4 tablespoons cocoa
1 tablespoon plus 1 teaspoon vinegar
1/2 cup oil
1 1/3 cups water
1 1/2 teaspoons vanilla

Directions

1. Sift all dry ingredients together into an 8x12-inch Pyrex baking pan.
2. Add vinegar, oil, water and vanilla.
3. Mix with a fork until blended.
4. Bake for 25 to 30 minutes at 350° F.
5. Cool and frost with Sugar and Cream Icing.

Sugar and Cream Icing Ingredients

1/3 cup margarine
3 ounces cream cheese
1/2 pound powdered sugar
1/2 teaspoon vanilla
1/2 cup chopped pecans

Directions

1. Cream margarine with cream cheese.
2. Stir in powdered sugar, vanilla and pecans.
3. Chill slightly before frosting cake.

Serves 8 to 10

Tomato Soup Cake (for real!)

This is a great cake for fall—the color is so reminiscent of autumn and Thanksgiving.

CAROLYNNE CHUNG

Ingredients

⅓ cup butter
1 cup white sugar
2 egg yolks
2 cups flour
¼ teaspoon salt
1½ teaspoons baking powder
1 teaspoon baking soda
1 teaspoon allspice
1 teaspoon nutmeg
1 teaspoon cinnamon
1 can condensed tomato soup
1½ cups raisins
½ cup walnuts, chopped (optional)

Directions

1. Grease and flour a 9-inch square baking pan.
2. Cream butter; add sugar and egg yolks.
3. Mix flour, salt, baking powder, baking soda and spices together.
4. Gradually add dry ingredients alternately with the tomato soup to the butter mixture.
5. Fold in raisins and, if desired, nuts.
6. Spread batter in prepared pan.
7. Bake at 350° F for about 50 minutes.

Suggestion: Double the recipe and bake in a large springform pan. This cake has a heavy pound-cake texture and, baked in a springform pan, it freezes beautifully and slices well.

Blueberry Pie

SANDRA WEZOWICZ

Ingredients

¾ to 1 cup sugar (personal preference)
⅛ teaspoon salt
¼ cup water
3 tablespoons cornstarch
4 cups blueberries, divided
1 tablespoon butter
2 teaspoons lemon juice
1 pie crust, baked and cooled
Whipped cream

Directions

1. Combine first five ingredients in a saucepan and cook over medium heat, stirring constantly.
2. When sauce boils, thickens and appears clear, remove from heat and stir in butter and lemon juice.
3. Cool and fold in 2 cups of blueberries.
4. Pour into baked pie crust and top with whipped cream.

Coconut Angel Pie
JANE HANSEN

Ingredients
4 egg whites
¼ teaspoon salt
1 teaspoon vinegar
1 cup sugar, plus 2 tablespoons
1 teaspoon vanilla
1 cup shredded coconut, browned
1½ banana
1 cup whipping cream

Directions
1. Beat egg whites until frothy and stiff.
2. Add salt and vinegar, and beat until stiff.
3. Gradually add sugar, beating after each addition.
4. Bake at 275° F for 1 hour. Let cool.
5. Just before guests arrive, sprinkle half of the coconut on the meringue crust. Lay banana slices on top. Add 2 tablespoons sugar to whipping cream and whip. Spread the whipping cream over the top and sprinkle remaining coconut over it. Refrigerate for 1 hour.

Glazed Peach Pie
Even if it falls apart a little when serving, it'll taste awesome anyway!
GRETCHEN FINCH MAHONEY

Ingredients
4 to 5 cups ripe fresh peaches, peeled and sliced
½ cup water
1 cup sugar
3 tablespoons plus 2 teaspoons cornstarch
1 tablespoon butter
⅛ teaspoon almond flavoring
1 9-inch pie shell, baked and cooled
Whipped cream

Directions
1. Blend enough sliced peaches in blender to make just 1 cup peach puree.
2. Add water, sugar and cornstarch to peaches in blender. Blend until well mixed and smooth.
3. Slice the rest of the peaches into pie shell until quite full.
4. Cook blended mixture over medium heat, stirring with a wire whisk until it bubbles and thickens and turns translucent. Stir in butter and almond flavoring.
5. Pour carefully over pie. With the tip of a table knife, coax mixture down between peach slices. Be sure all peaches are covered with glaze.
6. Chill in refrigerator for at least 4 hours.
7. Cover with whipped cream before cutting and serving.

Oreo Mud Pie
WANDA HANSEN

Ingredients

⅓ cup butter or margarine, melted
24 Oreo cookies, crushed
Ice cream
1 can of your favorite fudge topping
1 pint Cool Whip

Directions

1. Combine butter and cookies and press ⅔ of the mixture into a 9x13-inch baking pan.
2. Freeze for 1 hour.
3. Slice ice cream into ¾-inch slices and place over cookie crust. Smooth slices together. Freeze again for 1 hour.
4. Pour fudge topping evenly over ice cream. Freeze again.
5. Top with a layer of Cool Whip.
6. Sprinkle top with reserved cookie mixture. Freeze 4 to 6 hours.

Tips: Chocolate mint ice cream is so good in this recipe! Peppermint candy ice cream is a good choice to use for Valentine's Day.

Shortbread Cookies
CAROLYNNE CHUNG

Ingredients

2 cups white flour
1 cup confectioners' sugar
1 cup cornstarch
¼ to ½ teaspoon salt
1½ cups soft butter (not margarine)
1 teaspoon almond flavoring

Directions

1. Combine dry ingredients in a bowl.
2. In a separate bowl, combine butter and almond flavoring and gradually knead with dry mixture. Continue kneading to get air out.
3. Roll with rolling pin to desired thickness (a thicker cookie tastes better and does not burn as quickly or crumble).
4. Cut with cookie cutter.
5. Bake at 300° F until done (barely tan color).

Note: Dough can be wrapped in a food storage bag and refrigerated or frozen until ready to use. Allow time to warm up slightly before rolling out.

Peach Custard Pie

JANE HANSEN

Ingredients
1 pie shell, unbaked
2 cans freestone peaches, drained
¾ cup sugar
3 tablespoons flour
¾ cup whipping cream
½ teaspoon cinnamon

Directions
1. Arrange peaches in pie shell.
2. Mix together sugar and flour and sprinkle over peaches.
3. Pour whipping cream over fruit and sprinkle with cinnamon.
4. Bake at 450° F for 10 minutes; reduce heat to 350° F and continue to bake for 30 minutes.

Fruit Crumble
(no refined sugar)

DENISE FRANGIPANE

Crumb Crust Ingredients
1 cup almonds, hazelnuts or pecans
2 cups flour
½ cup date sugar, brown sugar or Sucanat
½ cup (1 stick) butter, softened but not melted

Filling Ingredients
½ cup honey
2 tablespoons granulated tapioca (or 2 tablespoons flour)
4 to 6 cups fruit (any combination of blueberries, peaches, nectarines, prunes, plums, etc.)

Directions
1. Preheat oven to 375° F.
2. Lightly toast nuts (chop, slice, sliver or grind nuts).
3. In a large bowl, mix together nuts, flour and sugar.
4. Cut in butter until mixture looks like coarse crumbs.
5. Press one-half mixture into the bottom of a 9-inch baking dish.
6. In medium bowl, mix honey and tapioca.
7. Gently fold in fruit and pour over crust.
8. Sprinkle remainder of flour mixture over fruit.
9. Bake until topping is golden and filling is bubbly (approximately 40 minutes).
10. Cool 10 to 20 minutes.

Suggestion: Top with a scoop of fresh whipped cream or ice cream.

Special Pumpkin Pie

This is a different version of pumpkin pie that will leave you wanting more. It melts in your mouth.

JANE HANSEN

Pie Ingredients
1 pie shell, baked and cooled
1 pint vanilla ice cream, softened
1 cup canned pumpkin
1¼ cup sugar
½ teaspoon nutmeg
½ teaspoon ginger
½ teaspoon salt
½ teaspoon vanilla
1 cup whipping cream

Directions
1. Spread the ice cream in the pie shell. (I use a little more than 1 pint and I let it sit out for several minutes, so it is more spreadable.)
2. Mix together the canned pumpkin, sugar, nutmeg, ginger, salt and vanilla.
3. Whip the cream and fold it into the pumpkin mixture.
4. Pour the pumpkin mixture over the ice cream and freeze overnight.

Sauce Ingredients
1½ cups brown sugar
½ cup white corn syrup
½ cup butter
½ cup cream
1 teaspoon vanilla

Directions
1. Combine the sugar, corn syrup and butter; heat to melt the sugar and bring the mixture almost to a boil, but don't let it actually boil.
2. Add the cream and vanilla.
3. Serve warm over a sliver of pie.

Southern Pecan Pie

This is a dessert you can put together quickly if you keep the ingredients on hand for unexpected guests.

CECI SHEETS

Ingredients
3 eggs, slightly beaten
1 cup sugar
1 cup dark Karo corn syrup
2 tablespoons margarine, melted (do not use low-fat light margarine)
1 teaspoon vanilla
1¼ cup pecans
1 9-inch unbaked or frozen deep-dish pie crust

Directions
1. Preheat oven to 350° F.
2. In a large bowl, stir the eggs, sugar, corn syrup, margarine and vanilla until blended.
3. Stir in pecans. Pour into pie crust.
4. Bake in 350° F oven for 50 to 55 minutes or until knife inserted near center comes out clean.

Serves 8
Suggestion: Serve à la mode or with whipped cream.

Blueberry Boy Bait

BARBARA JAMES

Ingredients
2 cups flour
1½ cups sugar
2 teaspoons baking powder
1 teaspoon salt
⅔ cup butter, softened
1 cup milk
2 eggs
1 cup blueberries (preferably fresh), rinsed and drained
¼ cup sugar
½ teaspoon cinnamon
Ice cream or whipped cream (optional)

Directions
1. In a large bowl, combine flour, sugar, baking powder, salt, butter, milk and eggs.
2. Blend with mixer at low speed until moistened; continue to beat at medium speed for 3 minutes.
3. Pour into a greased and floured Pyrex dish.
4. Arrange blueberries on top.
5. Combine sugar and cinnamon; sprinkle over top of blueberries.
6. Bake at 350° F for 40 to 50 minutes.
7. Top with ice cream or whipped cream, if desired.

Tip: This is so delicious, it may not need a topping!

Mary's Friend Bernice's Pound Cake
MARY LANCE SISK

Cake Ingredients

1½ cups shortening

3 cups sugar

6 eggs

1 cup milk

3½ cups flour, sifted

1 teaspoon salt

½ teaspoon lemon flavoring

½ teaspoon vanilla flavoring

Directions

1. Cream shortening and sugar together until light and fluffy.
2. Add eggs two at a time, beating well after each addition.
3. Add milk and flour alternately, making sure that you begin and end with the flour. Add salt and flavorings.
4. Grease and lightly flour a 15-inch tube pan and pour the batter into it.
5. Bake at 325° F for 1 hour and 25 minutes or until cake tests done.

Glazed Lemon Sauce Ingredients

5 tablespoons lemon juice

5 tablespoons orange juice

2½ cups confectioners' sugar

Directions

1. Mix ingredients together and pour over cake.
2. Return cake to the oven for about three minutes.

Texas Pecan Pie
CAROL TORRANCE

Ingredients

¼ cup butter or margarine

½ cup sugar

¾ cup white Karo syrup

¼ cup pure maple syrup

3 eggs, slightly beaten

1 teaspoon vanilla

2 cups pecan halves

1 9-inch pie shell, unbaked and chilled

Directions

1. Preheat oven to 350° F.
2. Stir butter with spoon until creamy; add sugar slowly and continue to stir until light.
3. Slowly stir in Karo and maple syrups.
4. Add eggs and vanilla; stir to blend.
5. Fold in nuts and pour into pie shell.
6. Bake in 325° F oven for 1 hour.
7. Cool and serve.

Fresh Fruit Crepes
RHONNI GREIG

Crepe Ingredients
1¼ cups flour
2 tablespoons sugar
4 eggs
1½ cups milk
1 teaspoon vanilla
½ teaspoon salt
1 tablespoon vegetable oil

Directions
1. Put all ingredients into a blender. Blend until combined and smooth.
2. Refrigerate for at least 2 hours or mix and refrigerate overnight.
3. Re-blend batter slightly when ready to use.
4. For a large crepe, pour a small amount into a pan that is at least 10 inches in diameter (I use a nonstick frying pan).
5. Swirl batter around so it coats the bottom and then cook until bottom is lightly browned. Gently remove from pan and fill with the fresh fruit and additional items listed below.

Filling Ingredients
1 small carton of cottage cheese
1 small carton of nonfat yogurt
2 or 3 baskets of fresh berries (strawberries, blueberries, raspberries) or 4 or 5 sliced peaches
1 can of whipped cream, or 1 pint whipping cream, whipped

Directions
1. Place crepe on a plate. Place a line of cottage cheese and a line of yogurt in the middle. Spoon the fresh berries or peaches on top of the cottage cheese and yogurt.

2. Roll crepe and top with another line of yogurt and a line of whipped cream.

Suggestion: Top with another spoonful of fresh fruit and whipped cream, if desired.

When entertaining, I use fresh flowers
from our yard in centerpieces.
We always tell our guests that children are
welcome; I see it as opportunity to bless
families. People are more important than
things; so when chili gets spilled on a white
couch, or dishes and glasses get broken,
it is cleaned up and forgotten.
I can't stand the thought of nice dishes
staying in the cupboard all year and only
being brought out for so-called special
people. I use the good dishes frequently.

RHONNI GREIG

Pumpkin Date Nut Torte
CAROLYN SUNDSETH

Ingredients

¾ cup oil (canola is my choice)
16-ounce can of pumpkin
2 cups brown sugar
2 teaspoons vanilla
4 eggs
1 cup flour
1 teaspoon soda
1 teaspoon baking powder
1 teaspoon cinnamon
1 teaspoon nutmeg
½ teaspoon ginger
1 cup nuts, chopped (I use walnuts.)
1 cup dates, chopped, mixed with 2 tablespoons flour

Directions

1. Preheat oven to 350° F. Grease and flour a 9x13-inch baking pan.
2. Blend oil, pumpkin, brown sugar, vanilla and eggs.
3. Mix dry ingredients together and beat into pumpkin mixture.
4. Fold in nuts and dates.
5. Pour into prepared pan and bake for 30 minutes or until a toothpick comes out clean.

Note: You can substitute pumpkin pie spice for the cinnamon, nutmeg and ginger.

Suggestion: Serve warm or cool with whipped cream or ice cream.

Hershey Bar Squares
NANCY McGUIRK

Ingredients

1 cup Crisco shortening
1 cup brown sugar
2 cups flour
1 teaspoon vanilla
1 small bag chocolate chips
½ cup milk
1 cup chopped walnuts

Directions

1. Blend first four ingredients together and press out on a cookie sheet.
2. Bake at 350° F for 10 minutes or until golden brown
3. Melt chocolate chips with milk to a spreading consistency. Spread on warm base and sprinkle with chopped walnuts.
4. Cut into squares to serve.

Quick and Cool Lemon Pie
CECI SHEETS

Ingredients

1 can sweetened condensed milk
½ cup Realemon Lemon Juice
3 cups Cool Whip
Yellow food coloring
1 graham cracker crust
Lemon curl

Directions

1. Mix together the condensed milk, Realemon Lemon Juice and Cool Whip until creamy.
2. Add about 10 drops of yellow food coloring and stir well.
3. Pour into graham cracker crust.
4. Place a lemon curl in the center and refrigerate for two hours.

Serves 6

Buttermilk Cake
ESTHER BURROUGHS

Ingredients

½ cup shortening
½ cup margarine
3 cups sugar
½ teaspoon salt
5 eggs, separated
⅓ teaspoon baking soda
1 tablespoon hot water
1 cup buttermilk
3 cups flour
1 teaspoon vanilla

Directions

1. Grease and flour a 9x13-inch pan.
2. Cream together the shortening, margarine, sugar and salt.
3. Add egg yolks, one at a time.
4. Add baking soda to hot water; then add this to ½ cup buttermilk.
5. Add flour to shortening mixture alternately with buttermilk (use all of the buttermilk); add vanilla and mix.
6. Beat egg whites until stiff and fold into batter.
7. Pour into prepared pan and bake at 325° F for 1 hour and 15 minutes.
8. Let cool and then turn out onto platter.

Serves 24

Suggestion: This tastes wonderful served with strawberries and ice cream, or serve toasted and buttered with tea.

Chocolate Log
This makes a beautiful Christmas dessert.
MARILYN REY

Ingredients
1 pint whipping cream
¼ cup sugar
1 teaspoon vanilla
1 package Nabisco Famous Chocolate Wafers
Cherries (optional)

Directions
1. Whip the cream until stiff.
2. Fold in sugar and vanilla.
3. Spread each wafer with whipped cream.
4. Arrange wafers in a "log" held together and frosted with whipped cream.
5. Chill several hours or overnight.
6. Cut log in diagonal slices so that each piece looks like a many-layered torte.
7. Garnish each slice with a cherry, if desired.

Christmas Variation: Make log as described above. Then cut a 3-inch piece diagonally off the end of the log and attach it to the side (diagonally cut side against log) so that it resembles a branch of a tree. Decorate with maraschino cherries and sliced almonds, colored green. (Put a few drops of green food coloring and 2 drops of water in a small jar. Add almonds and shake until almonds turn green.)

Gingerbread and Apple Fluff Topping
THETUS TENNEY

Ingredients
1 box gingerbread mix
1 regular size jar of applesauce, chilled
1 small carton Cool Whip or 1 carton whipping cream, whipped
Powdered sugar
Pink or yellow food coloring
Red or green cherries (optional)

Directions
1. Bake gingerbread according to recipe; let cool.
2. Empty jar of applesauce into mixing bowl.
3. Mix with Cool Whip or whipping cream that has been whipped to a stiff consistency.
4. Sweeten to taste with powdered sugar. (Powdered sugar has less tendency than table sugar to thin topping.)
5. Tint with food coloring.
6. Cut gingerbread in squares, slice each piece open, and put on individual serving plates.
7. Remove top half of sliced gingerbread squares and put a heaping tablespoon of topping onto bottom half.
8. Replace top half and then add another heaping tablespoon (or more) of topping onto top half.
9. A red or green cherry makes a pretty garnish.

International Recipes

A Glimpse of Other Cultures

Traveling is always a wonderful and enriching adventure, and these pages are an opportunity to enjoy a very long trip as we make a bridge to other countries through sharing recipes.

Being a part of an international ministry has allowed me the privilege of experiencing various cultures and customs around the world. I have seen the Great Wall of China, the pyramids of Egypt and the Taj Mahal of India. They are indeed wonders of the world. Yet as magnificent as these sights are, they are just structures. What makes a culture memorable is the heart and soul of the people themselves.

Being invited into a person's home always makes a culture come alive in a way that viewing a mere structure cannot. There is a heart connection that takes place as you sit around a table with one another to share a meal.

In Hebrews 13:2 we are encouraged "to entertain strangers, for by so doing some have unwittingly entertained angels."

As you read through the following pages, you will find not only recipes from around the world but also various ways that each culture extends hospitality and a wonderful feeling of friendship that bonds hearts forever. And who knows . . . you may just find yourself entertaining an angel!

International Breads

Chappatis—India
MERINA NETTO

Ingredients
2 cups chappati (whole wheat) flour
¾ teaspoon salt
1 tablespoon oil
Water
Butter

Directions
1. Knead flour with salt, oil and enough water to form a soft elastic dough.
2. Divide dough into equal parts, each about the size of a small lemon.
3. Roll each part thin like a tortilla and cook it on a flat iron pan.
4. Flip it over on both sides so that it cooks but does not burn.
5. Continue to cook until the chappati is light brown in color.
6. Serve with a little butter.

India is a vast country with 26 states. Food habits, customs and even languages vary from state to state; but warmth, love and hospitality are common to Indian people. Though space was always a bit of a problem for us, we entertained despite the lack of room. We simply opened up the neighbor's home in order to create more room to accommodate guests.

MERINA NETTO

Moist Scones—Great Britain

There is nothing more British than midafternoon tea served to friends or neighbors at a social gathering.
One of the favorite items at such a tea is scones with cream and jam.

WINIFRED ASCROFT

Ingredients

8 ounces (2 cups) self-rising flour
4 ounces (1 cup) strong plain flour
4 ounces hard shortening (butter or margarine)
4 ounces (½ cup) sugar
Pinch of salt
1 large egg, beaten, plus extra
4 fluid ounces (½ cup) milk, plus extra

Directions

1. Place the flours and shortening into a mixing bowl and stir until mixture becomes like bread crumbs.
2. Add the sugar and salt and stir together.
3. Add the beaten egg and milk to the mixture and stir until it is mixed to a soft consistency.
4. Turn the dough mixture out onto a floured surface and roll to ¾-inch thickness.
5. Cut into rounds with a pastry cutter and place on a lightly greased and floured cookie sheet.
6. Brush the tops with milk or beaten egg and bake at 160° C (325° F) for about 25 minutes, until lightly brown.
7. Cool until slightly warm; then split and spread with jam.

Suggestion: Put a large spoon of whipped cream on top of each scone and serve with hot tea. (English tea is always made with boiling water.)

Note: Two ounces of currants or raisins may be added to the mixture as an alternative to cream and jam, if desired. Serve with butter when adding currants or raisins.

Diet Roll—Finland
This cake is gluten free, lactose free and fat free.
KRISTINA TURNER

Cake Ingredients

3 eggs
1½ dl (½ cup) sugar
¾ dl (¼ cup) potato flour
⅓ dl (2 tablespoons) cocoa powder
1 teaspoon baking powder

Filling Ingredients

2 bananas, mashed
3 dl (1 cup) berries

Directions

1. Beat eggs and sugar together well.
2. Mix flour, cocoa powder and baking powder and add to the eggs.
3. Pour the mixture on a baking plate (jelly roll pan) that is lined with baking paper.
4. Bake in the oven for 5 minutes at 250° C (475° F).
5. Turn cake gently out of baking plate onto another baking paper covered with a little sugar.
6. Gently peel the paper away from the underside of the cake.
7. Mix bananas and berries and pour over the cake.
8. Roll the cake in the baking paper and let it stand and cool for several hours.
9. Cut in slices before serving.

Kitchen Style

What's your style in the kitchen?
I just thought I'd ask.
Are you steady and tidy
Or drippy and fast?
Are you "aproned" or daring,
With spatter-splashed clothes?
Do you batter your fingers
And flour your nose?
Do you like to make small talk
Or stick to the task?
Do you measure exactly?
I just thought I'd ask.

Do you stir up your favorites
Or risk something new?
Do you keep a towel handy
Or clean when you're through?
Do you mind if you're watched by
A cat or a child?
Do you use spices subtly
Or do you go wild?
Have you ever made biscuits
As tough as a tire?
Have you peeked in your oven,
Discovered a fire?

Do you hum while you're dicing?
Or sip on some tea?
Do you scrape off your beaters
Or lick—privately?
Do you use every bowl and
Your counter's last spot?
Do you cook like your momma
Or are you self-taught?
When you mix up some cookies
How long will they last?
What's your style in the kitchen?
I just thought I'd ask.

—Deena Wilson

International Soups

Goulash Soup—Hungary
LILLA GERE

Ingredients

1 medium onion, diced
1 tablespoon vegetable oil
1½ pounds beef or pork, cubed
Salt, pepper and paprika to taste
2 tomatoes, chopped
1 green pepper, chopped
6 cups water, divided
1 pound potatoes, cut into cubes
2 carrots, sliced
1 stalk of celery with two leaves (put in whole)
2 sliced parsnips with the greens (put in whole)
1 handful of thin short noodles

Directions

1. Sauté onion in oil until transparent.
2. Add meat, salt, pepper, paprika, tomatoes and green pepper.
3. Cook and stir until meat is browned and loses its liquid.
4. Add 2 cups water and cook until meat is half cooked.
5. Add about 4 more cups of water.
6. Add vegetables and noodles and cook until meat is completely done.
7. Add more seasoning, if needed.

Serves 4

Suggestion: Serve with fresh bread or cheese biscuits.

Cream of Zucchini—Belgium
A quick recipe when you are too busy to prepare an elaborate meal.
MONIQUE VANDEN BLOOCK

Ingredients

4 zucchini
Water to cover
Salt and pepper to taste
¼ pound (½ cup) cream or less (about 100 cl. in Europe is 20 to 35 percent fat)
Grated cheese (optional)

Directions

1. Peel the zucchini and cut in thick slices.
2. Put in a pan and just cover with water (you can always add more if needed).
3. Let them cook until tender (about 20 minutes).
4. Mix zucchini with a mixer until texture is soft and smooth. Season with salt and pepper.
5. Place in a soup bowl. Add cream in the soup bowl or serve it in a little milk jar.
6. Sprinkle with grated cheese, if you like.

Pounded Olo Yam with Spinach Egusi Soup—Nigeria

BISI ADELUYI

Yam Ingredients

1 medium-sized olo yam
2 litres water to boil

Directions

1. Peel yam, cut in required sizes. Boil, cooking until yam is soft enough for pounding (mashing), about 25 minutes.
2. Pound (mash) and portion into the traditional calabash (2- to 3-quart) dish and serve with hot vegetables.

Soup Ingredients

8 medium-sized fresh tomatoes, ground (chopped)
4 medium-sized fresh pepper, ground (chopped)
1 large onion, ground (chopped)
Water
1 pound of bush meat (beef), cooked
1 medium-sized stockfish (cod or any bottom fish), cooked
4 medium-sized snails, washed
1½ liters (5¼ cups) water
2 tablespoons of crayfish, ground (chopped)
20 medium shrimp
2 Maggi cubes (bouillon)
Spinach leaves, washed and shredded
3½ cups of egusi (ground melon seed)
1 wrap of beniseed (iru)
2 cooking spoons of palm oil
Salt to taste

Directions

1. Wash and grind (chop) the vegetables; pour into pot and boil for 15 minutes.
2. Add the bush meat, stockfish and snails.
3. Add the water.
4. Add the crayfish, fresh shrimp and Maggi cubes.
5. Add the spinach leaves.
6. Add the ground egusi and iru wrap.
7. Add the palm oil.
8. Add salt.
9. Stir and simmer for 10 minutes.
10. Serve with pounded (mashed) yam.

Kumara and Spinach Soup—New Zealand
Janet Robertson

Ingredients

2 tablespoons butter

2 onions sliced

1 bunch spinach, washed and trimmed

1 litre (3¼ cups) chicken stock

500 g (16 ounces) kumara, peeled and diced (may substitute sweet potato)

Pinch of nutmeg, salt and pepper

1 cup canned coconut cream

Directions

1. Melt butter in a large saucepan; add onion and spinach and cook gently till onions are soft.
2. Add chicken stock; boil and skim fat off the top.
3. Add kumara with nutmeg, salt and pepper and simmer for 45 minutes.
4. Leave to cool before blending (or mashing with electric beater).
5. Before serving, reheat soup and add coconut cream to desired consistency.

Serves 4

Famous Split Pea Soup—Holland
Jannie Reverda

Ingredients

1 pound (450 grams) split peas

500 grams (1 pound) pork hocks

2.5 liters (½ gallon) water

150 grams (6 ounces) bacon

1 onion, chopped

Butter or margarine

1 celery root, chopped

4 leeks, chopped

Celery leaves, chopped

1 smoked sausage

Salt and pepper to taste

Fresh parsley, chopped

Directions

1. Boil the peas and pork. When boiling, turn the heat down low and skim the foam off the surface.
2. Add bacon; put the lid on the pan and cook slowly for 1 hour.
3. Fry the onion in butter or margarine until golden in color.
4. Add onion, celery root, leeks, celery leaves, sausage, salt and pepper to the soup.
5. Let it cook gently for 35 minutes. Remove the meat, bacon and sausage from the soup and crush the peas with a wooden spoon.
6. Before serving, sprinkle the parsley in the soup.
7. Serve the meat (with the bone), the bacon and the sausage sliced separately on a plate with a bowl of split pea soup.

Groundnut (Peanut) Soup—Ghana
DOROTHY DANSO

Ingredients

1½ kg (3 pounds) mutton or beef
1 large onion, chopped
Salt
200 g (7 ounces) tomato paste
12 cups of water, divided
1 cup groundnut (peanut) paste
2 teaspoons chili pepper

Directions

1. Clean and cut meat into bite-sized pieces and place in deep
   saucepan.
2. Add onions and 2 teaspoons salt to meat.
3. Steam for a few minutes and then stir in tomato paste.
4. Mix the groundnut (peanut) paste with 6 cups water and pour
   over steamed meat.
5. Reduce heat and continue to boil (do not cover pot, as it will
   boil over).
6. Add chili pepper, and salt to taste; add remaining 6 cups water.
7. Boil for 15 to 20 minutes; then simmer over low heat for
   1 hour or until you see signs of oil developing on surface of
   soup.

Serves 10

Suggestion: Serve with potato flour and fufu (farina) or boiled rice
or yam.

We Ghanaians are noted for our
warm reception and hospitality.
We always receive a visitor with
a smile and handshake and serve
water, even before conversation.
A visitor is officially
welcomed and then asked the
mission or purpose of the visit.
When the visitor leaves, it is
customary to always see them off
at the door or the gate.

DOROTHY DANSO

Food Preparation

- Remove butter and eggs from the refrigerator one hour before using them.
- To avoid tears when peeling onions, first put them in the refrigerator for 15 minutes.
- Onions will fry to a golden color without going black if you put them in flour before putting them in the frying pan.
- To whiten rice, put a few drops of lemon juice in the water while cooking.

- Chop herbs by hand at the last moment. Preferably, only mix herbs with cooked ingredients.
- To prevent fruit from soaking the dough in pies, sprinkle the bottom of the pie pan with corn flour, which will absorb the juices that ooze from the fruit.
- To avoid stuck-together ice cubes after removing them from their molds, immediately shower the cubes with sparkling water.

International Vegetables

Raita Salad—India
MERINA NETTO

Ingredients
1 cup yogurt
¼ teaspoon salt
½ teaspoon sugar
1 small green chili pepper, finely chopped
1 medium onion, chopped
2 to 3 tablespoons cilantro leaves, chopped
2 cucumbers, peeled and cubed
1 tomato, chopped (optional)

Directions
1. Beat yogurt with salt and sugar.
2. Add chopped green chilies, onion and cilantro leaves.
3. Add chopped cucumber and mix. Add tomato, if desired.
4. Serve chilled.

Umbhida Le Dobi (Spinach and Peanut Butter) —Zimbabwe
This is very nutritious but fattening. It is advisable to dish small portions as you cannot resist to finish what is on your plate.
EGGRINAH KALIYATI

Ingredients
2 bunches spinach
Boiling water
4 large onions or 6 medium onions, finely cut
6 large tomatoes, finely cut
Salt to taste
8 ounces (250 g) peanut butter

Directions
1. Wash and cut spinach, put in a pot and pour boiling water over it. Strain spinach and set aside.
2. Cook onions until soft and then add tomatoes, spinach and salt. Cook for a short time and do not allow spinach to lose its color.
3. Add peanut butter and mix with a wooden spoon until vegetables and peanut butter are completely mixed.
4. Simmer for a few minutes over low heat.

Suggestion: Serve with sorghum or cornmeal thick porridge (isitshwala).

Fatali (Sweet Potatoes with Nsinjiro) — South Africa
TOWERA MASIKU

Ingredients
3 cups sweet potatoes, cubed and slightly cooked
1 tomato, skinned and chopped
1 onion, chopped
½ cup nsinjiro (pounded groundnut flour) or peanut butter
Salt and pepper

Directions
1. Place the sweet potato pieces in a saucepan.
2. Add tomato and onion and cook gently for 5 minutes.
3. Add the nsinjiro and season to taste.
4. Cook for another 5 minutes.

Suggestion: Serve at once with a green salad.

Rösti (Swiss Potatoes) — Switzerland
Rösti is often called a potato pancake, but it is really Switzerland's original farmhouse breakfast.
A panful of golden Rösti with a cup of hot milky coffee makes a good start to a working day. However, now it is generally eaten at midday or in the evening.

JYTTE NIELSEN

Ingredients
Potatoes
Lard

Bacon Rösti: Add chopped onion and diced bacon.
Zurich Cumin Rösti: Add slivers of cheese.
Egg Rösti: Serve the Rösti with fried eggs on top.

Directions
1. Boil some potatoes (preferably waxy, not floury, ones) in their jackets.
2. The following day, skin and rub potatoes through a coarse grater.
3. Heat a knob of lard in a heavy frying pan, and when it is hot, put in the grated potato. Press down slightly with a wooden spoon and lower the heat. Fry gently until golden and then turn the cake and brown the other side. Add a little more fat if required. Serve piping hot.

Potato Dumplings—Germany

In southern Germany and Austria, dumplings are called knodel and are a popular side dish, especially for meat and gravy.

HANNELORE ILLGEN

Ingredients

1 kg (2.2 pounds) mealy or semimealy potatoes
80 to 150 g (½ cup) flour (amount depends on the
   potato starch)
2 eggs
¼ teaspoon salt
1 pinch of ground nutmeg
3 liters (10 cups) water
2 teaspoons salt
2 rolls or slices of toast
1 tablespoon butter

Directions

1. Cook the potatoes (with skins); peel them and immediately squeeze them and strew them loosely on a tray or work surface.
2. Sprinkle ⅔ of the flour over the potatoes.
3. Stir the eggs, salt and nutmeg together and add it.
4. Knead the potatoes until they become a dough (work quickly, so the dough doesn't get sticky).
5. Add as much flour as needed, so the dough is not too damp.
6. Form a roll about 1 inch in diameter with your hands.
7. Bring the water to a boil and add the salt.
8. Dice the rolls or toast and fry them in the butter.
9. Cut the dough-roll in 2-cm (1-inch) slices.
10. Flour your hands and form dumplings. Put a few cubes of toast into the middle of each dumpling.
11. Drop the dumplings into the softly boiling water, boil them up once and then, with the lid off, cook them over low heat for about 20 minutes or until done. The dumplings are done if they rise to the surface. They should be shiny on the outside and fluffy on the inside. Take them out of the water with a skimmer and let them drain.

Champ—Ireland

ISOBEL SMITH

Ingredients

2 pounds boiled potatoes
1 cup scallions (spring onions)
1 cup hot milk
Salt and pepper to taste

Directions

1. Peel and mash potatoes.
2. Add scallions, milk and seasoning.
3. Beat until light and fluffy.

Suggestion: Serve with plenty of butter.

Joff Beans—Nigeria
BISI ADELUYI

Ingredients

1 cup of Joff (brown) beans
4 liters water
4 medium-sized red peppers
6 medium-sized tomatoes
1 medium-sized onion, ground (chopped)
2 pounds meat
2 tablespoons crayfish
20 medium shrimp
½ pound dried fish
2 cooking spoons of palm oil
2 Maggi cubes (bouillon)
Salt to taste

Directions

1. Pick the stones from the beans; then wash the beans and add water.
1. Bring to a boil and cook for about 1 hour or with a pressure cooker for 30 minutes.
3. Add peppers, tomatoes, tartashe, onions (ground).
4. Add the meat, crayfish, shrimp and dried fish.
5. Add palm oil and Maggi cubes.
6. Add salt.
7. Stir and simmer for 20 minutes.
8. Serve hot.

Aludum (Potato Curry)—Nepal
SHANTI ADHIKARI

Ingredients

2 pounds potatoes, peeled and cut into chunks
⅓ to ½ cup vegetable oil
A few dry chilies
2 large onions, chopped
½ pound tomatoes, cubed
50 grams (1¾ ounces) ginger
2 cloves garlic
Yellow curry powder
Chili powder
Salt to taste

Directions

1. Boil the potatoes.
2. Heat frying pan, add oil and fry a few chilies only until brown.
3. Add onion and cook just until lightly brown.
4. Add the tomatoes.
5. Stir in ginger, garlic, curry powder and chili powder.
6. Add potatoes and salt; mix, cover and cook over low heat. Check from time to time to see if a bit of water is necessary.
7. Serve when potatoes are well cooked.

Masamba Otendera (Green Vegetables with Pounded Groundnuts, or Peanut Butter) — Southeast Africa

TOWERA MASIKU

Ingredients

½ cup water
Pinch of salt
2 handfuls of sweet cabbage leaves, chopped
2 tomatoes, chopped
1 onion, chopped into small pieces
½ cup nsinjiro (pounded groundnut flour, or peanut butter)

Directions

1. Boil water, add salt and then the chopped leaves, tomatoes and onions.
2. Simmer for 7 to 10 minutes.
3. Add the nsinjiro (or peanut butter) to flour.
4. Cook until tender.

Suggestions: Instead of sweet cabbage, use any fresh vegetable like pumpkin leaves, turnip leaves, bean leaves, etc. Serve with rice or grits.

Whenever we are serving, to show courtesy, we kneel down to honor our guest(s).

TOWERA MASIKU

Bannock Cakes and Bearberry Jelly

It was the book on Pilgrim recipes and customs that got me started one Thanksgiving. I wondered, *If I were a Pilgrim woman in this strange new land called America, what would I be cooking up as I dirtied every pot and pan in my kitchen?* And that is how my two young sons and I found ourselves experimenting. After washing out an empty milk jug, we followed an authentic Pilgrim recipe for making swizzle, a popular drink of water, molasses, white vinegar and ginger that ended up looking a little like something that might have leaked from, say, a carburetor.

"Ughhh!" Three-year-old Ethan took a brave sip, screwed up his face and gave a full-body shudder. I had to agree. Swizzle lacked one thing: a Mr. Yuck poison-control sticker. But the Pilgrims loved this cooling beverage, so said the book. I believe that if I had been a Pilgrim and had spent my day splitting fence rails or stirring a steaming tub of laundry in the baking sun, I, too, could have acquired a taste for swizzle. We rolled up our sleeves and moved on to the next Pilgrim recipe, bannock cakes.

These pancakes, browned in butter, were a lot easier than swizzle to swallow. Made of stone-ground cornmeal, eggs and not a whole lot more, bannock, or johnnycakes, were an every-meal mainstay of the Pilgrim diet. I mixed, my husband fried, and the boys blew on them to cool them for sampling. We all agreed they were pretty tasty, especially the butter part. These pancakes could get my vote for breakfast . . . and also for ballast. Just a few of them under your belt and you would never, ever blow away in a high New England wind. If I had been a Pilgrim, would I have tried to think up 1,001 creative ways to serve my family bannock cakes? You bet. Because when the wheat, rye and barley crops all died, bannock cakes were the heaven-sent manna that helped fill big and little Pilgrim tummies.

The next recipe—a whole baked pumpkin stuffed with apples—looked too daunting for us, and I didn't happen to have any bearberries (cranberries) on hand to give bearberry jelly a whirl. My six-year-old turned thumbs down on the lima beans in succotash stew. A recipe for hot nuts sounded easy but not too exciting. So we plopped four hard-boiled eggs into a glass jar of beet juice and watched them pickle themselves pink. Pickled eggs aren't my favorite, but if I had been a Pilgrim, I have a feeling I would have remembered to thank God for such simple daily blessings—eggs from my own chickens and the freedom to offer thanks in my own way.

At our family Thanksgiving gathering that year, we felt very authentic as we trooped into my sister-in-law's home, carrying the traditional green bean casserole with little fried onions on top and swizzle, bannock cakes and pickled eggs. Various family members took polite, thimble-sized sips of swizzle. Others tentatively nibbled the edges of bannock cakes like field mice before fleeing back to Pepsi and the appetizer tray. There was only one taker for our pickled eggs—the patriarch of the family. He took a bite, lifted a shaggy white eyebrow and proclaimed, "Pretty good!" We took into account that he'd been a missionary for years and probably had long ago perfected the fine art of swallowing the unknown and declaring "Pretty good" (maybe in several languages).

As for me, my taste for things Pilgrim made me feel a little closer to my American roots that Thanksgiving. As I pushed away from our turkey feast with all the trimmings and relaxed with family in the safety and comforts of home, I felt in a new way that it was all much more than just "pretty good." I felt very full, very humbled . . . and very, very thankful.

—Deena Wilson

International Entrées

Surprise Luncheon—Germany
HANNELORE ILLGEN

Ingredients
Small potatoes
A variety of fruits and vegetables—whatever your fridge has to offer
Cheese, diced, or cold cuts
Frozen fish fillets
Butter

Directions
1. Clean the potatoes and bake them (with or without skins) for 30 minutes.
2. Arrange the selection of fruits and vegetables colorfully on as large a silvery plate as possible.
3. Don't be shy! Slices of cucumber can be arranged next to pieces of tangerine, slices of bananas can be placed next to tomato halves, and don't mind cherries being close to lettuce. If fresh fruit is not available, you can used canned fruit.
4. Diced cheese or little rolls of cold cuts can be put in between; radishes and strips of sweet pepper add extra color.
5. Frozen fish fillets can be quickly fried in butter.

Suggestion: Serve with various dips, homemade yogurt or crème fraîche and spices.

Deep-Fried Chicken—Nepal
SHANTI ADHIKARI

Ingredients
2 pounds chicken meat
2 cloves garlic, minced
2 teaspoons salt
4 tablespoons soy sauce
2 cups vegetable oil

Directions
1. Cut meat into small pieces and place in bowl with garlic, salt and soy sauce.
2. Mix well and let stand for 15 to 30 minutes.
3. Pour oil into a deep pan and heat, but do not allow oil to smoke.
4. Add a small amount of the meat at a time to the hot oil and fry until brown. Leave on low heat to cook for approximately 10 minutes.
5. When it is cooked, take it out and put the next bit in; continue until all the meat has finished cooking.

Six Hungry Men—Zimbabwe
Eggrinah Kaliyati

Ingredients

Water for beans
1 kg (2 pounds 3 ounces) sugar beans
1 kg (2 pounds 3 ounces) boro steak
3 medium-sized onions
2 tablespoons vegetable oil
4 large tomatoes, sliced
Salt and pepper to taste

Directions

1. Soak beans overnight; wash and boil slowly until soft.
2. Cut meat into cubes and fry until slightly brown.
3. Cut onions and fry in oil; add tomatoes and meat to this mixture.
4. Strain water from the beans and put beans into casserole dish.
5. Add meat mixture to beans in casserole dish.
6. Add salt and pepper and mix well.
7. Add one cup of water if necessary.
8. Cover and bake in a moderate oven until meat and beans are cooked.

Suggestion: Serve with rice or boiled potatoes.

When you entertain, make your home look beautiful and welcoming. Embrace your guests if it is your custom. If you greet by a handshake, give a tight grip, as this will make your guest feel welcome. Family members should be congenial and never quarrel when there are guests.

Eggrinah Kaliyati

Guinea Fowl in Rich Grape Sauce—France
MALVINE EVENSON

Ingredients
1 knob butter
1 tablespoon oil
1 guinea fowl, jointed
2 shallots, chopped
6 tablespoons port wine
9 tablespoons light double cream
1 clove garlic, crushed in its skin
1 sprig thyme
Salt and pepper to taste
1 bunch large white grapes, skinned

Directions
1. Heat butter and oil together in large frying pan over low heat and brown the pieces of guinea fowl.
2. Add the chopped shallots and port wine.
3. Coat the pieces of fowl with cream; add the clove of garlic and thyme; season with salt and pepper.
4. Transfer all the ingredients into an oven dish; cover with foil and cook in hot oven (220° C or 425° F) for 40 minutes.
5. In the last 5 minutes, add the grapes.

Serves 4

Macaroni Caprice—Hong Kong
JACKIE SIMMONS

Ingredients
8 ounces macaroni
Water for macaroni, plus 1 cup
2 tablespoons olive oil
1 pound ground beef
2 large onions, finely chopped
1 clove garlic, crushed
8 ounces liverwurst, chopped (gives a great flavor)
2 cups tomato, fresh or canned, chopped
1 tablespoon tomato paste
2 teaspoons salt
½ teaspoon mixed herbs
¼ teaspoon black pepper
½ cup grated cheese

Directions
1. Cook macaroni; drain and set aside.
2. Fry ground beef in oil until browned.
3. Add onions and garlic. Cook together 10 minutes.
4. Add liverwurst, tomatoes, tomato paste, seasonings and 1 cup water.
5. Simmer 20 to 30 minutes.
7. Fold in the macaroni and place in a casserole dish.
8. Sprinkle with cheese and bake in a moderate oven until cheese is well melted.

Suggestion: Serve with French bread and tossed salad.

Fribourg Bénichon Lamb—Switzerland

The great Thanksgiving festival of the Bénichon (blessing) at the end of the summer is held in the Canton of Fribourg. The dish, which must be on every table, is a savory lamb stew with raisins. It is served with mashed potatoes and cooking pears, which are stewed whole without peeling.

JYTTE NIELSEN

Ingredients

2 tablespoons oil
1 kg (2 pounds) boned shoulder of lamb,
  cut in 2-inch (6 cm) chunks
Pepper
Flour for dredging
1 onion
4 cloves
1 leek, chopped
1 stick of celery, chopped
4 ounces (½ cup) red wine
½ liter (2 cups) beef stock
Bay leaf, sprigs of sage, and thyme
2 garlic cloves, crushed
4 ounces (½ cup) seedless raisins
Salt to taste

Directions

1. Heat oil in a heavy saucepan or casserole dish.
2. Pepper the meat well and dredge with flour.
3. Stick the cloves into the onion, and fry meat rapidly with the onion until it is well browned.
4. Add the leek and celery and fry for about 2 minutes.
5. Pour in the wine, mix well, and add beef stock, spices, garlic and raisins.
6. Simmer for 2 hours or until the meat is really tender.
7. Salt at the last minute.

Stir-Fried Beef and Vegetables—Australia
JOAN MORTON

Ingredients

¼ pound French beans or fresh beans
½ can water chestnuts
1 or 2 stalks of celery
Boiling water
Cold water
5 teaspoons soy sauce
1 teaspoon sugar
1 tablespoon saki or dry sherry
1 pound rump or round steak, cut into fine strips
1½ teaspoons corn flour
3 to 4 tablespoons oil for frying
1 clove garlic, crushed
1 stick ginger, chopped
1 teaspoon sesame seed oil (optional)
½ bunch spring onions, chopped in 1-inch pieces
1 handful fresh mushrooms, sliced thinly
Salt to taste

Directions

1. Cut beans in pieces, slice water chestnuts, and slice celery.
2. Plunge beans and celery into boiling water for 1 minute; drain and rinse in cold water.
3. Combine soy sauce, sugar, saki or sherry, beef and corn flour. Allow to stand for a few minutes.
4. Heat 2 tablespoons of oil in pan; add half of the garlic, ginger and sesame oil.
5. Discard garlic and ginger when brown. Add all vegetables and salt.
6. Stir-fry for a few minutes; remove and set aside.
7. Add remaining oil, garlic and ginger. Discard garlic and ginger when brown. Add beef marinade and stir-fry 3 to 4 minutes. While cooking, beef will make juice.
8. Return vegetables to beef and stir-fry long enough to heat vegetables through.

Ground Beef and Potato Casserole—Holland
JANNIE REVERDA

Ingredients
Butter
1½ pounds chopped beef
Salt, pepper and nutmeg to taste
5 large onions, chopped
3 tablespoons warm water
Vinegar
Worcestershire sauce
2 kilos (4 pounds) potatoes
Water
1 beef-tea cube (bouillon)
1 egg

Directions
1. Melt the butter in a frying pan till slightly brown.
2. Add the chopped beef and stir until brown; season with salt and pepper and nutmeg.
3. Add chopped onions and fry them with the meat.
4. Mix 3 tablespoons warm water with vinegar and Worcestershire sauce and add this mixture slowly into the pan and stir carefully; simmer for 3 hours.
5. Peel the potatoes, cut them into small pieces and boil in water with a little salt and beef-tea cube.
6. When done, pour off the water, add the egg and a lump of butter.
7. Mash the potatoes and season with salt and pepper.
8. Butter a casserole dish, pour the contents of the frying pan into the dish and top with the mashed potatoes.
9. Put some butter on top of the mashed potatoes and put the dish into a preheated oven until the top is lightly brown.

Suggestion: Serve with homemade applesauce.

Quiche—New Zealand
Janet Robertson

Ingredients

3 eggs
1 cup milk
½ cup flour
½ teaspoon baking powder
1 onion, chopped small and cooked
1 clove of garlic, crushed
2 rashers (strips) bacon, precooked and chopped small,
  or 1 tin corned beef
1 cup spinach, cooked
2 potatoes, cooked and cubed
1 cup tasty cheese (try sharp cheddar or Swiss), grated
1 teaspoon Maggi Onion Soup
1 teaspoon Maggi Green Herb Stock Powder
Salt and pepper to taste
Parsley or slices of tomato

Directions

1. Beat eggs, milk, flour and baking powder just to combine.
2. Add cooked onion, garlic, bacon, spinach, potatoes, cheese and seasonings and herbs.
3. Pour into greased casserole dish or flan dish and cook at 400° F for 30 minutes.
4. Garnish with parsley or slices of tomato (or a garnish of your choice).

Serves 8

Chicken in Cream—Guatemala
Gladys Harshbarger

Ingredients

2 chickens (fryers)
2 teaspoons salt
1 cup sour cream (100 percent sour cream without fillers)
Chopped green pepper (optional)

Directions

1. Cut chicken into pieces; if you like, remove skin.
2. Put chicken in a pot, add the salt and half the sour cream. DO NOT COVER.
3. Cook over low heat uncovered for 10 to 15 minutes; add the rest of the sour cream and continue cooking. Add green peppers, if desired.

Note: Do not cover the pot, as this will make the chicken watery. The chicken will cook, if young, in about ½ hour or so. If you want more gravy, you can add more sour cream. Stir once in a while with a wooden spoon.

Suggestion: Serve with boiled or mashed potatoes, mixed vegetables or green peas.

Chicken Mulligatawny—Sri Lanka
Sylvia Weerasinghe

Ingredients
1 large chicken
1½ pints cold water
¼ ounce coriander seed
⅛ ounce sweet cumin seed
¼ ounce white cumin seed, ground and divided
Pinch of ground turmeric
¼ teaspoon fenugreek
1 tablespoon red onions, sliced
2 cloves garlic, chopped
2 slices green ginger, chopped
1 2-inch cinnamon stick
Small sprig curry leaves
4 medium-sized ripe tomatoes, sliced
Salt to taste
½ pint thick coconut milk
Drippings
Lime juice

Directions
1. Cut chicken into joints and put in saucepan; add water and simmer for 30 minutes.
2. Add the coriander and the sweet cumin after grinding it with ⅛ ounce white cumin seed.
3. Add the turmeric, fenugreek, half the onion, garlic, ginger, cinnamon stick, curry leaves, tomatoes and salt.
4. Boil until chicken is tender.
5. Strain off the stock and put the best pieces of chicken back into the stock.
6. Mix remaining white cumin with the coconut milk and add to stock.
7. Heat the drippings in a frying pan and add the remaining onions. When browned, add to the stock.
8. Add lime juice and salt and bring to a boil.

Suggestion: Serve with cooked rice.

Chicken Adobo in Coconut Milk—Philippines
Celia Espiritu

Ingredients
1 chicken, cut in serving pieces
1 head garlic, crushed and chopped
1 cup vinegar
Salt and pepper to taste
1 cup coconut cream powder dissolved in 2 cups water

Directions
1. Marinate chicken in garlic, vinegar, salt and pepper.
2. Place in a skillet and simmer slowly until tender.
3. Dissolve coconut cream powder in water and add. Boil until desired thickness of coconut cream sauce is attained.

Meat Cutlets—Sri Lanka

SYLVIA WEERASINGHE

Ingredients

1 pound ground meat
¼ pound small bread pieces or mashed potatoes
1 tablespoon onions, finely chopped
1 teaspoon fennel, chopped
Salt and pepper
Powdered cloves
Cinnamon
Juice of one lime
1 egg, lightly beaten
1 egg, slightly beaten
Bread crumbs

Directions

1. Put meat, bread or potatoes, onion and fennel in a bowl and mix well.
2. Season to taste with salt, pepper, cloves and cinnamon; and mix well.
3. Add lime juice and bind with lightly beaten egg.
4. Divide mixture into 12 equal portions and form into round balls.
5. Dip into slightly beaten egg and roll in bread crumbs.
6. Fry them in the meat drippings until they are nicely browned.
7. Drain well and serve.

A common greeting of the Sri Lankans when they welcome guests for a meal is "Welcome, Welcome! It is nice that you accepted the invitation. Hope you will enjoy this time with us."

SYLVIA WEERASINGHE

Chicken Birvani—India
MERINA NETTO

Ingredients

4 medium onions, thinly sliced, divided
2 pounds chicken, chopped
1 teaspoon salt, plus extra for seasoning
1 teaspoon garlic, crushed
1 teaspoon ginger, crushed
½ teaspoon garam masala (can substitute allspice powder), divided
1 cup clarified butter, or oil
1 cup yogurt
1 can tomato sauce
1 teaspoon cayenne pepper
1 tablespoon chopped cilantro leaves
1 to 2 small green hot peppers chopped
2 cups rice
5 cups water
1 teaspoon cumin seed
2 or 3 bay leaves
1 teaspoon poppy seeds, soaked in water and ground
Juice of one lemon
Red and yellow food coloring
Tumeric color
⅛ teaspoon saffron

Directions

1. Fry 3 of the 4 onions to a dark brown color and set aside.
2. Cook chicken with the remaining onion, 1 teaspoon salt, garlic, ginger and half of the garam masala until about three-quarters done.
3. Add 3 tablespoons butter or oil, yogurt, tomato sauce, cayenne pepper, cilantro leaves and green hot peppers. Cook on low heat until the liquid is thick.
4. While chicken is cooking, wash and soak rice for 30 minutes.
5. Cook rice in 5 cups of water with cumin seed, remaining garam masala, salt to taste and bay leaves and poppy seeds until three-quarters done.
6. Drain rice and add the lemon juice; return to the cooking pot.
7. In a deep baking dish, use 3 to 4 tablespoons butter or oil to coat the bottom and sides of dish.
8. Arrange half the rice, then the chicken and the remaining rice.
9. Finally, add the brown fried onions.
10. Mix a little red and yellow food coloring, also the tumeric color and saffron, and sprinkle the colors here and there on the rice.
11. Cover with a tight-fitting lid or with aluminum foil, and bake at 300° F for 30 minutes.

Suggestions: You can decorate with golden currants and fried cashew nuts. Serve hot with an Indian pickle (you can purchase the pickles at an international food store) and a Raita Salad (see index).

Haddock, Vegetables and Cheese Bake—Iceland
EDDA SWAN

Ingredients

2 cups instant rice or partially cooked rice

250-300 grams frozen vegetable mixture (such as peas, carrots and corn)

800-1000 grams haddock fish fillets, cut into serving-sized pieces

Small amount of lemon juice

1 6-8 ounce can of crushed pineapple, drained, with 1 tablespoon juice reserved

1½ cups mayonnaise

2 tablespoons mustard

1-2 teaspoons garlic powder

1-1½ teaspoons curry powder

½-1 teaspoon paprika

Slices of cheese (Swiss, mozzarella or other good cheese)

Directions

1. Mix rice and frozen vegetables; place half of the mixture in a glass baking dish, covering the bottom of the dish.
2. Place the fish fillets on top of the rice and vegetable mixture.
3. Squeeze a small amount of lemon juice over the fish.
4. Repeat another layer of rice and vegetables.
5. Top with crushed pineapple.
6. Mix mayonnaise (enough to cover the fish) with 1 tablespoon pineapple juice and vegetables.
7. Top with slices of cheese.
8. Bake uncovered for approximately 30 minutes at 350° F.

Traditional Irish Stew—Ireland
ISOBEL SMITH

Ingredients

2 pounds mutton or stewing lamb

1 pound carrots, thinly sliced

1 pound onions, thinly sliced

Salt and pepper to taste

3 pounds potatoes, sliced

1½ pints stock or water

Directions

1. Cut meat into neat pieces and trim off fat.
2. In a saucepan, arrange layers of meat, carrots, onions, seasoning and potatoes.
3. Add stock or water just to cover; simmer gently for 2 hours.

Fish Menudo—Philippines
CELIA ESPIRITU

Ingredients

2 pounds fish fillets, cubed
½ teaspoon salt
¼ teaspoon pepper
2 teaspoons lemon juice
2 teaspoons soy sauce
4 cloves garlic, crushed
1 onion, chopped
¼ cup oil
1 cup potatoes, diced
1 cup carrots, diced
1 cup tomato sauce
½ cup green peas
1 red pepper, cut in strips
½ cup water

Directions

1. Marinate fish in salt, pepper, lemon juice and soy sauce.
2. Sauté garlic and onion in oil.
3. Add potatoes, carrots and tomato sauce.
4. Add fish, including marinade.
5. Add remaining vegetables and water.
6. Simmer until potatoes are done.

Roasted Leg of Lamb—Oman
MOYA MICHALAKIS

Ingredients

1 leg of lamb
1 garlic bulb, ground
1 teaspoon meat spices
½ teaspoon cumin, roasted and ground
½ teaspoon coriander, roasted and ground
Salt to taste
Lemon juice to taste
½ cup vinegar
Banana leaves or aluminum foil

Directions

1. Using a knife, slice deep pockets in the meat.
2. Combine the garlic with the spices. Mix with the lemon juice and vinegar.
3. Rub the meat with the mixture and marinate for 5 hours or overnight.
4. Wrap the seasoned meat in banana leaves or aluminum foil.
5. Bake in oven to desired doneness.

Laham Bil Khal (Meat with Vinegar) —Oman
MOYA MICHALAKIS

Ingredients
Cinnamon
Cardamom
Dates
Water
Tamarind
Meat
Garlic

Directions
1. Crush together cinnamon and cardamom.
2. Soak dates in water; remove pits and then knead.
3. Soak tamarind in water; knead well and sift.
4. Cut meat into small cubes.
5. Rinse meat and add tamarind, date molasses and garlic.
6. Heat the mixture, stirring frequently until meat is well cooked (add water while cooking if necessary).

Suggestion: Serve with bread.

Black-Eyed Beans Stew—Ghana
DOROTHY DANSO

Ingredients
6 ladles (tablespoons) palm (red) oil or cooking oil
1 large onion
6 large fresh tomatoes, blended
Pepper, salt and chili pepper
2 tins of canned fish
4 cups black-eyed beans, boiled

Directions
1. Heat oil in saucepan.
2. Add sliced onion and sauté for 1 minute.
3. Add tomatoes; add pepper and salt to taste.
4. Allow to simmer for 10 minutes or until sauce becomes thick.
5. Add canned fish and simmer for 1 minute.
6. Add beans and allow to cook over low heat for another 5 minutes. Add chili pepper and additional salt to taste.

Serves 6

Suggestion: Serve with fried ripe plantain and boiled rice.

Mutton Palak (Mutton Spinach) —India
MERINA NETTO

Ingredients

2 10-ounce packages of frozen spinach or 2 bunches fresh spinach
1¼ teaspoons salt, divided
2½ cups water, divided
1 tomato, chopped
1 small green chili
1-inch piece ginger
½ cup oil
1 teaspoon ginger paste
1 teaspoon garlic paste
3 medium-sized onions, finely chopped
1 pound mutton or lamb, chopped into bite-sized pieces
½ teaspoon turmeric
½ teaspoon ground red pepper
½ teaspoon garam masala (allspice powder)
3 tomatoes, blanched and chopped
½ cup yogurt
½ cup fresh cream

Directions

1. Wash spinach, boil with ½ teaspoon salt and water.
2. Drain and squeeze out water.
3. Blend spinach in a blender with tomato, green chili and ginger.
4. In a medium-sized saucepan, heat oil and fry ginger and garlic pastes and onion until brown.
5. Add mutton pieces and fry well; then add turmeric powder, red pepper powder, garam masala, tomatoes, salt and yogurt.
6. Mix well and fry over medium heat until the oil separates.
7. Add two cups of water and cook over low heat until mutton is tender.
8. Add ground spinach mixture, and fry until oil separates.
9. Add cream just before serving.

Suggestion: This dish goes well with chappatis, an Indian unleavened bread (see index).

Zurich Sliced Veal—Switzerland

This is one of the great dishes of European cooking. It is not difficult, but you must work swiftly. In Zurich it is always served with Rösti, but plain boiled rice or pasta may be substituted.

JYTTE NEILSEN

Ingredients

1½ pounds veal, thinly sliced and cut into bite-sized pieces
2 tablespoons butter
1 onion or 2 shallots, chopped
Salt and pepper to taste
4 ounces (½ cup) dry white wine
8 ounces (1 cup) cream
Small piece of lemon peel, chopped
Parsley, chopped

Directions

1. Fry veal quickly in butter until golden.
   Reserve on a hot dish.
2. Fry chopped onions or shallots lightly. Season well.
3. Add wine and simmer until sauce reduces to about half, stirring constantly.
4. Add cream and heat, but do not boil.
5. Add meat and lemon peel to sauce. Mix ingredients, heat through and serve at once, garnished with parsley.

Variation: Fry ½ pound mushrooms in an extra tablespoon of butter with the onion.

Suggestion: Serve with Rösti (see index).

Swedish Meatballs and Gravy—Sweden

Below, you will find a basic recipe for a prime component of the Swedish smorgasbord. As time goes by, you will find that you add a little bit of this and a little bit of that, and suddenly you have your very own specialty. But ask any Swedish man and he will say "Nothing is like Mama's meatballs."

ANITA NORDSTROM

Meatball Ingredients

1 pound ground beef
Tomato ketchup, Worcestershire sauce, paprika,
　soy sauce, etc. for flavoring
Salt and black or white pepper
2 tablespoons bread crumbs
1 egg
¾ cup water or milk
1 onion
2 potatoes, boiled and cooled

Directions

1. According to taste, add tomato ketchup, Worcestershire sauce, paprika, soy sauce, salt, pepper, etc. to the ground beef.
2. Mix bread crumbs in egg and water or milk. Let bread crumbs swell together in the egg and water.
3. Peel the onion and potatoes and cut or grind them up really fine.
4. Mix onion and potatoes into egg mixture, and add ground beef and mix well.
5. Fry a small ball for taste; if necessary, add more flavorings and spices.
6. Make little balls and brown them. Be careful not to get the pan too hot.

Gravy Ingredients

2 tablespoons butter
1½ cups hot water
2 tablespoons flour
2 tablespoons cool water
Salt and pepper to taste

Directions

1. Melt 2 tablespoons of butter in the pan.
2. Add 1½ cups hot water.
3. Blend 2 tablespoons of flour with some water and pour slowly into the pan, stirring constantly.
4. Add salt and pepper and let boil for approximately 5 minutes.

As a guest in a home in Sweden you will, most of the time, find a nicely set table with flowers and candles. Even a housewife with a thin pocketbook tries to do that.

ANITA NORDSTROM

Perfect Caribbean Pelau—Trinidad

ANNETTE COOMBS

Ingredients

2 pounds chicken
1 tablespoon lime juice
2 packs Tastemakers, chicken flavor
3 tablespoons coconut milk powder
1 cup warm water
4 tablespoons browning liquid (Kitchen Bouquet), divided
2 cups water
2 tins processed pigeon peas
1 whole green hot pepper
2 cups rice
1 cup chopped pumpkin
1 medium carrot, peeled and cubed

Directions

1. Clean chicken and cut into small pieces. Season with lime juice and one pack Tastemakers. Set aside.
2. Blend coconut milk powder with warm water. Set aside.
3. In a heavy saucepan, add seasoned chicken and two tablespoons browning liquid. Heat and stir until evenly browned, and cook for one minute.
4. Add water, coconut milk, two tablespoons browning liquid and one pack Tastemakers to liquid in saucepan. Bring to a boil. Add pigeon peas and green hot pepper.
5. Add rice to boiling liquid. Stir. Add pumpkin and carrots. Bring to the boil; cover saucepan lightly and reduce heat. Cook for 30 minutes.
6. Remove hot pepper.

Serves 6 to 8

Suggestion: Serve with coleslaw or green salad.

Comfort Food

When our second son, Ethan, was born, he came with a mixed-up timer. He was his cutest and most alert from about midnight to 6:00 A.M. Dawn was the inevitable cue for his little lavender eyelids to flutter and droop. While my husband and I carried on animated conversations with him, squeaked tiny toys and jiggled him desperately, he went limp and drifted into happy hibernation. A week of all-nighters and we were so exhausted we were dazedly tossing dirty diapers in the dresser drawer and pitching clean towels in the diaper pail.

My mom flew in from Ohio to help. She began to rock and cuddle, diaper and reassure. One morning—or was it evening?—I found her at the dining room table, leafing through a stack of my cookbooks. She said something like, "I thought I'd make a little something."

"Hummpryjgh," I mumbled as I propped myself against the nearest wall, in my not-so-clean bathrobe. I had no clue whether there was anything resembling an egg or a carton of milk in the refrigerator. I wasn't even sure I could locate the refrigerator. No matter. My mom began quietly moving about in my kitchen, ready to stir, measure and improvise. I retreated gratefully to the bedroom, but I know just the way her finger tapped its way down the recipe as she worked, searching for and discovering the measuring cups, the flour, the spatula, the vanilla. The sounds rising from the kitchen were as reassuring as a promise: the ring of a spoon on the edge of a bowl, the rhythmic whir of the mixer,

the clink of baking pans, the oven door squeaking open and shut. Before long a cloud of sweet aroma lured me back into the kitchen.

On my blue china platter sat a fragrant ring of something unspectacular but in every way wonderful, especially for a peanut-butter lover. Peanut-butter cupcakes with peanut-butter frosting. I was almost embarrassed by the little thrill of anticipation I felt as I reached for one. "Oh, Mom, these are delicious!" I was not too embarrassed to bite into another one without hesitation. And, I think, another. When was the last time I had eaten, anyway? Six weeks ago? "These are mine," I told myself giddily, eyeing both the platter and my mom, and brushing crumbs from my chin. "Yes, all mine."

Over the next few days, I did have some foods from other major food groups, I'm sure. And like a big girl, I'm certain I must have shared some cupcakes—but not many. I feasted on them, amazed that something so simple could seem so sustaining. At a crazy time when it seemed that my body, my days, my nights and my life were suddenly, strangely, not mine, "a little something" turned out by the same hands that had once cradled a little someone soothed my soul. Those weren't just peanut-butter cupcakes Mom offered. They were comfort food at its best—edible hugs.

—Deena Wilson

International Desserts

Black Fruitcake—Trinidad

Trinidad's traditional Black Fruitcake can be used for celebrations, weddings, anniversaries or festivals as a cake beautifully frosted. Garnish with pudding to suit the occasion, and bake with charms if used as a Christmas dessert.

ANNETTE COOMBS

Ingredients

½ pound currants, minced
½ pound raisins
½ pound sultanas, minced
½ pound seeded prunes
½ pound cherries, cut into small pieces
¼ pound mixed peel, chopped fine
1 bottle (25 ounces) grape juice
2 ounces almonds, finely chopped
¼ pound brown sugar
¼ cup hot water
½ pound flour
2 teaspoons baking powder
½ teaspoon powdered cinnamon
½ pound fresh butter
½ pound fine brown sugar or granulated sugar
½ teaspoon vanilla extract
6 eggs

Directions

1. The day before making the cake, mince together currants, raisins, sultanas, seeded prunes, cherries and mixed peel; pour grape juice over all. Blend. Cover the bowl and let stand. (The fruit can be soaked weeks in advance, but more grape juice will be required.) Blend fruits thoroughly with almonds.

2. Butter and prepare for steaming large cake pans or large pudding molds; if cake is to be baked, line the pan or mold with 3 layers of greased paper.

3. Put ¼ pound brown sugar into strong-bottomed aluminum or iron pot; heat, stirring briskly until it liquefies and becomes dark golden in color.

4. Remove from heat and add hot water, stirring briskly.

5. Return to heat. Blend until there is an even consistency. Remove from heat and cool.

6. The caramel coloring should be thick, but it must be able to pour. A little more hot water may be added, if necessary. Set aside.

7. Sift flour, baking powder and cinnamon together four times.
8. Cream butter and beat in sugar gradually. Continue until sugar grains are dissolved and mixture is light and fluffy.
9. Add vanilla and blend well.
10. Stir dry mixture into butter mixture.
11. Add caramel coloring to fruit and fold fruit into butter mixture.
12. Whip eggs until light and thick enough to form a ribbon when beater is withdrawn. Cut and fold into mixture. Add a little flour if mixture shows signs of curdling.
13. If cake is to be baked: Turn mixture into prepared pans or molds and bake in slow oven, 300 to 325° F for about 2 hours.
14. If cake is to be steamed: Fill molds ⅔ full. Put on covers; place molds on trivets or stands in pot containing boiling water that comes halfway up around the molds. Keep water at boiling point; add boiling water as needed. Remove from steamer and set in cold water for a few seconds before turning out of mold. Set in oven a few minutes to dry a little.

Tip: For a Christmas dessert, pour half the mixture into each pan or mold and arrange charms around the edge and in the center. Then pour in the remainder of the mixture.

I cap my lunches or dinners with a basket of fresh fruit, in addition to the dessert and coffee. I follow this with heated rolled-up hand towels for each guest. I wet the towels and scent them with cologne (heat 30 seconds on high in the microwave). The result is a fragrant, hot, refreshing hand wash right at the table. My guests enjoy the comfort this brings!

CELIA ESPIRITU

Cherry and Almond Cake—Great Britain
WINIFRED ASCROFT

Ingredients

8 ounces (1 cup) sugar
8 ounces (1 cup) margarine
3 eggs, slightly beaten
8 ounces flour (2 cups, not self-rising)
½ cup milk
2 teaspoons almond essence, or flavor, to your taste
  (cake should have a delicate almond flavor)
4 ounces almonds, ground
Pinch of salt
4 to 6 ounces glacéed cherries, halved
Flour

Directions

1. Line the bottom of a deep 8-inch round cake pan with baking paper; set aside.
2. Beat sugar and margarine together until creamy.
3. Add the eggs and flour alternately into the mixture, stirring until completely blended.
4. Stir in the milk and almond essence followed by the ground almonds and the salt.
5. Lastly, lightly roll the glacéed cherries in flour to prevent them from sinking in the cake mixture, and add them to the mixture.
6. Do not overbeat this mixture; it is not a light sponge cake.
7. Pour into prepared cake pan.
8. Bake for 1¼ hours at 275° F, or 130° C. Cake may need to bake an additional 15 minutes.

Tip: This cake keeps well and is best stored for 5 days before cutting into it.

To make my guests feel welcomed at very special dinners, I scatter some jasmine flowers around the dinner plates. My guests delight at their fragrance all evening. Lilacs or gardenias will have the same appeal.

CELIA ESPIRITU

Danish Butter Cake—Denmark
TOVE MOMMER

Vanilla Cream Ingredients
2 egg yolks
1 tablespoon sugar
2 teaspoons flour
¾ cup milk
½ teaspoon vanilla extract

Butter Filling Ingredients
5 tablespoons icing sugar
5 ounces (⅔) cup butter

Dough Ingredients
9 ounces (2 cups) flour
6 ounces (¾ cup) butter
50 g fresh yeast (or 3 packages of dry active yeast)
3 tablespoons heavy cream
1 egg
1 tablespoon sugar

Icing Ingredients
1 cup icing sugar
water or sherry

Directions
1. To make vanilla cream: Beat egg yolks with sugar, flour and milk. Cook over low heat while beating the whole time until thick. Remove from heat and add vanilla extract; then cool, stirring occasionally to keep vanilla cream smooth.
2. To make butter filling: Cream icing sugar and butter together to form a smooth cream for the butter filling. Set aside.
3. To make dough: Sift flour into a mixing bowl. Add butter and rub it into the flour with your fingertips until the mixture resembles fine bread crumbs.
4. Crumble the fresh yeast into the cream. Beat the egg and sugar into the yeast mixture and pour this mixture over the flour. Mix all the ingredients together quickly. Don't overwork the dough or it will become tough.
5. Preheat the oven to 225° C (400° F).
6. On a lightly floured surface, roll out half of the dough into a large circle about 10 inches (25 cm) in diameter. Place the dough in a 9-inch buttered tin, covering the bottom and extending up the sides of the pan. Spread the vanilla cream on the bottom.
7. Roll out the other half of the dough in a long rectangle and spread the butter filling on it.
8. Roll the dough up and cut in slices. Lay the slices on the vanilla cream, cut side up. Let the cake rise 30 minutes in a cool place. Brush the cake with egg and bake 30 to 40 minutes.
9. To make icing: Mix icing sugar with a little water or sherry to make a thick icing.
10. Serve each slice of cake with a dab of icing.

Bedouin Delight (Date Ice Cream) — Oman
MOYA MICHALAKIS

Ingredients
6 egg yolks
60 g (2 ounces or ¼ cup) Caster sugar
480 ml (1 pint) milk

Date Paste
90 g (3 ounces) dried dates, soaked in cold water, drained
   and crushed

Directions
1. Beat egg yolks and sugar until light lemon color.
2. Bring the milk to a boil and pour into the egg mixture,
   beating constantly.
3. Return the mixture to the saucepan and reduce the heat,
   continuing to stir until mixture thickens. Do not boil.
4. Remove from heat and continue to stir until cool.
5. Process in an ice cream freezer or freeze and beat at hourly
   intervals until the proper consistency is reached. When nearly
   ready, add the date paste and complete the freezing process.

Serves 6

Suggestion: Serve by putting two or three scoops of ice cream in
a large glass, pouring over the ice cream one Arabic-coffee-sized
cup of Omani coffee, sprinkling with dried fruit (chopped apricots, raisins, toasted almond flake—enough for a mixed handful per person) and decorating with whipped cream.

Trifle—Ireland
This is a wonderful dessert served with a spot of tea.
ISOBEL SMITH

Ingredients
1 package small sponge cakes
1 can fruit of your choice, juice reserved
1 small jar jelly
1 pint fresh cream
1 package Hundreds & Thousands (little colored balls)

Directions
1. Place sponge cakes in the bottom of a dish.
2. Place fruit over sponge cakes.
3. Spoon jelly over fruit and add juice of fruit.
4. Whip cream and spoon over other ingredients.
5. Cover top with Hundreds & Thousands.
6. Chill several hours before serving.

Rice with Milk—Guatemala

I like to add raisins while this is cooking—also a twist of lemon peel. Some like to serve it for breakfast hot, like cereal.

GLADYS HARSHBARGER

Ingredients
6 tablespoons rice, uncooked
1 stick cinnamon
2 cups water
2 cups milk, divided
5 tablespoons sugar
Pinch of salt

Directions
1. Wash rice.
2. Cook rice with the cinnamon stick in 2 cups of water and 1 cup milk.
3. Cook until rice is soft, about 30 minutes.
4. Add 1 cup milk, the sugar and a pinch of salt.
5. Cook approximately 3 minutes more.
6. Serve hot or cold.

Serves 3

Fruit Salsa—Hong Kong

JACKIE SIMMONS

Ingredients
2 pints fresh strawberries
2 kiwi fruit
2 oranges
1 large apple
1½ tablespoons brown sugar
1 teaspoon vanilla

Directions
1. Process all the ingredients in a food processor just until finely chopped but still having texture. Do not overprocess.

Suggestion: Serve with plain cheesecake or over ice cream.

Rhubarb Dessert—Iceland
EDDA SWAN

Ingredients
400 to 500 grams (1 pound) fresh or frozen
  rhubarb, cut in small pieces
2 eggs, slightly beaten
¼ cup flour
1¼ cups sugar
1 scant cup flour
¾ cup brown sugar
2 ounces (¼ cup) butter

Directions
1. Grease an ovenproof dish.
2. Stir together rhubarb and eggs.
3. Mix together flour and sugar and stir into rhubarb mixture.
4. Pour into a greased baking dish.
5. Mix together flour, brown sugar and butter until crumbly. Crumble over the rhubarb mixture.
6. Bake at 200° C (375 to 400° F) for about 45 minutes.

Suggestion: Serve with whipped cream or vanilla ice cream and coffee.

Our form of greeting in Iceland is special because the word used when we greet someone is the word "blessing." We say "Komdu blessud og sael" to a female and "Komdu blessadur og saell" to a male.

This means "Come and be blessed and happy."

EDDA SWAN

Tarte Tatin—France
MALVINE EVENSON

Filling Ingredients

4 ounces (½ cup or 100 g) butter
4 ounces (½ cup or 100 g) sugar
6 large apples, sliced

Pastry Ingredients

8 ounces (2 cups or 200 g) flour
Pinch of salt
4 ounces (½ cup or 100 g) butter
3 to 4 tablespoons of water (enough to make dough)

Directions

1. Heat butter and sugar in 12-inch flan case (fluted pan); then add sliced apples.
2. Cook apples for 10 minutes over moderate heat.
3. Cook in oven for 5 minutes at 200° C (400° F). Set aside.
4. Sift flour and salt.
5. Rub the butter into the flour until it is well blended.
6. Gradually add sufficient water to make dough.
7. Roll out the dough and spread it on top of apples in flan case.
8. Bake in oven 200° C (400° F) for 20 minutes.
9. When the pastry is golden, take out of the oven and flip the pastry and apples over onto the serving dish. The apples will now be on top.

Serves 6

Pumpkin Pudding—Zambia
ELIZABETH DAKA

Ingredients

3 eggs, slightly beaten
1 cup pumpkin
½ cup sugar
¼ teaspoon orange rind, grated
1 12-ounce can evaporated milk
½ teaspoon cinnamon
¼ teaspoon allspice

Directions

1. Combine eggs and remaining ingredients. Mix until smooth.
2. Pour into 8 custard cups or a casserole dish.
3. Place in pan of hot water and bake at 350° F for about 40 minutes, until firm.
4. Cool before serving.

Serves 8

Suggestion: Serve with whipped cream or ice cream.

White Christmas—Australia
JOAN MORTON

Ingredients

1 cup powdered milk
1 cup mixed fruit
2 cups rice bubbles (Rice Krispies)
1 cup coconut
1 cup icing sugar (confectioners')
8 ounces Copha (solidified coconut oil) or vegetable shortening
Vanilla to taste

Directions

1. Put all ingredients except Copha into a bowl.
2. Melt Copha until lukewarm. Pour over dry ingredients.
3. Place in a jelly-roll pan, chill and cut into squares.

Salalah Cake (Pawpaw, Banana and Coconut)—Oman
MOYA MICHALAKIS

Ingredients

½ cup (125 g) butter
¾ cup Caster sugar (a little finer crystal
  than granulated sugar)
2 eggs
½ cup banana (1 banana), mashed
½ cup fresh pawpaw (could substitute apple, pear
  or guava), finely chopped, and a few thin slices
1½ cups self-rising flour
½ cup desiccated coconut
¼ cup milk
Icing sugar

Directions

1. Grease and line with paper a 20-cm round pan.
2. Beat butter and sugar until pale in color.
3. Beat in eggs, one at a time.
4. Stir in banana and pawpaw.
5. Stir in flour, coconut and milk; mix well.
6. Spoon into prepared pan.
7. Bake in moderate oven for 1 hour.
8. Let cool for 5 minutes and remove from pan to cooling rack.
9. Serve sprinkled with icing sugar.
10. Garnish with a few thin slices of pawpaw on top, overlapping like petals.

Serves 10

Tarts—Switzerland

The delectable tarts to be seen throughout the country are made in round, shallow tart pans on which the fruit, or other filling, is prettily arranged. There are many subtle variations which make all the difference to the appearance and to the taste.

Jytte Nielsen

Ingredients for Pastry
1 cup flour
Pinch of salt
Scant teaspoon baking powder
½ cup unsalted butter or vegetable shortening
Cold water

Directions
1. Mix flour, salt and baking powder; rub in butter or vegetable shortening.
2. Add enough cold water to bind to a stiff paste.
3. Roll out to fill a 10-inch tart pan.

Apple Tart
Peel and core apples and cut into thin slices. Arrange to overlap each other, following the rim of the plate in circles, narrowing to the center. Bake in a hot oven at 200° C (400° F) for 30 minutes. Strew sugar over the tart immediately after it is taken out of the oven to ensure crisp pastry.

Plum or Apricot Tart
Proceed as for apple tart, but cut the fruit in quarters. Spread two tablespoons ground almonds or hazelnuts, mixed with 1 tablespoon of brown sugar, on the crust before adding fruit.

Rhubarb Tart (Blueberry or Gooseberry Tart)
Use small pink sticks of rhubarb. Wash, skin and cut rhubarb into small chunks; scatter on pastry. Bake for 15 minutes. Beat 1 egg into ½ cup cream. Remove tart from oven, pour egg and cream mixture on the fruit, and bake for a further 15 minutes. This recipe is also used for blueberries and gooseberries.

Conversion Charts

Liquid Measures

Fluid Ounces	U.S.	Imperial	Milliliters
	1 teaspoon	1 teaspoon	5
¼	2 teaspoons	1 dessert spoon	7
½	1 tablespoon	1 tablespoon	15
1	2 tablespoons	2 tablespoons	28
2	¼ cup	4 tablespoons	56
4	¼ cup or ¼ pint		110
5		¼ pint or 1 gill	140
6	¾ cup		170
8	1 cup or ½ pint		225
9			250, ¼ liter
10	1¼ cups	½ pint	280
12	1½ cups or ¾ pint		340
15		¾ pint	420
16	2 cups or 1 pint		450
18	2¼ cups		500, ½ liter
20	2½ cups	1 pint	560
24	3 cups or 1½ pints		675
25		1¼ pints	700
30	3¾ cups	1½ pints	840
32	4 cups		900
36	4½ cups		1000, 1 liter
40	5 cups	2 pints or 1 quart	1120
48	6 cups or 3 pints		1350
50		2½ pints	1400

Solid Measures

U.S. and Imperial Measures		Metric Measures	
Ounces	Pounds	Grams	Kilos
1		28	
2		56	
3½		100	
4	¼	112	
5		140	
6		168	
8	½	225	
9		250	¼
12	¾	340	
16	1	450	
18		500	½
20	1¼	560	
24	1¼	675	
27		750	¾
32	2	900	
36	2¼	1000	1
40	2½	1100	
48	3	1350	
54		1500	1½
64	4	1800	
72	4½	2000	2
80	5	2250	2¼
100	6	2800	2¾

Oven Temperatures

Fahrenheit	Celsius	Gas Mark	Description
225	110	¼	Cool
250	130	½	
275	140	1	Very Slow
300	150	2	
325	170	3	Slow
350	180	4	Moderate
375	190	5	
400	200	6	Moderately Hot
425	220	7	Fairly Hot
450	230	8	Hot
475	240	9	Very Hot
500	250	10	Extremely Hot

Contributors

United States Ministries

KAY ARTHUR, Tennessee, is executive vice president and co-founder, along with her husband, Jack, of Precept Ministries. Kay is an internationally known Bible teacher, author and conference speaker and has written more than 20 books in addition to inductive Bible studies for Precept Ministries.

VONETTE BRIGHT, Florida, is cofounder of Campus Crusade for Christ Incorporated. Vonette is the wife of Dr. Bill Bright, founder and president of the campus movement dedicated to helping fulfill the Great Commission, with more than 20,000 godly men and women serving around the globe.

ESTHER BURROUGHS, Florida, is founder of Esther Burroughs Ministries, and has a national and international speaking and writing ministry to women.

DORIS BUSH, California, is the wife of Luis Bush, former president of AD2000 and Beyond, a ministry focused on world evangelization.

JEANNIE CEDAR, California, is married to Paul Cedar, president and CEO of Mission America, a coalition working to mobilize the church in America and share Christ with every person in this nation.

EVELYN CHRISTENSON, Minnesota, is a best-selling author and nationally known speaker. Her first book, *What Happens When Women Pray,* has sold 1 million copies.

MAJOR CAROLYNNE CHUNG, England, is an assistant adult and family ministries officer. The London headquarters serves the Salvation Army in the United Kingdom and the Republic of Ireland.

DENISE FRANGIPANE, Iowa, is the wife of Francis Frangipane, pastor, author and founder of Advancing Church Ministries.

CAROL GREENWOOD, Washington, is an author and speaker.

RHONNI GREIG, California, is the wife of Bill Greig III, president of Gospel Light.

ANNA HAYFORD, California, is married to Jack Hayford, founding pastor of The Church On The Way and chancellor and president of The King's Seminary.

SUZANNE HINN, California, is the wife of evangelist Benny Hinn, Benny Hinn Ministries.

ESTHER ILNISKY, Florida, is the founder of the Esther Network International Children's Global Prayer Movement. She is the author of *Let the Children Pray* (Regal Books).

CINDY JACOBS, Colorado, is cofounder and president of Generals of Intercession, an international intercessory prayer ministry that works with prayer leaders to help build prayer movements around the world. She is the author of *Possessing the Gates of the Enemy* (Chosen Books*), The Voice of God, Women of Destiny* and *Deliver Us from Evil* (Regal Books).

BARBARA JAMES, Oklahoma, is the Director of World Intercession Network with offices in Oklahoma City. WIN is a ministry seeking to encourage and motivate the Body of Christ at large to pray fervently.

DEE JEPSEN, Florida, is an author and speaker and served in the Reagan Administration as Liaison for Women's Organizations. She is currently a member of the Aglow International Board of Directors. Her husband is former Senator Roger Jepsen, from the state of Iowa.

LADY BIRD JOHNSON, Texas, is the wife of former president, Lyndon B. Johnson.

CAROLYN JONES, following a career of 20 years as a home economics teacher, is currently the Administrator of Global Missions at Westgate Chapel, Edmonds, Washington.

GRETCHEN FINCH MAHONEY, California, is the wife of Ralph Mahoney of World MAP (World Missionary Assistance Plan).

PATTI McGINNIS, Michigan, is the director of women's ministry, Calvary Church.

VIRGINIA OTIS, California, is the territory coordinator of Lydia Prayer Fellowship, California.

MARILYN TUCKER QUAYLE, Arizona, is the wife of former United States vice president Dan Quayle.

CECI SHEETS, Colorado, is the wife of pastor and author Dutch Sheets. He has written several books, including the best-selling *Intercessory Prayer* (Regal Books).

MARY LANCE SISK, North Carolina, is chairman of the National Coordinating Council for the Lighthouse Movement of Mission America, and chairman of the National Prayer Committee.

CAROLYN SUNDSETH, North Carolina, is a speaker and served in the Reagan Administration as Liaison for Women's Organizations.

THETUS TENNEY, Louisiana, is the author of *Prayer Takes Wings* (Regal Books) and is a regular contributor to *Spirit-Led Woman* and a member of the magazine's advisory board. Her husband is Rev. Tom Tenney, International Coordinator for World Network of Prayer.

KATHY TROCCOLI, Tennessee, is a songwriter and vocal recording artist. She is a Grammy and Dove Award nominee.

Aglow International

JANE HANSEN, Washington, serves as president and CEO of Aglow International, an outreach ministry that is impacting the lives of women in 135 nations. She travels extensively, sharing a message of God's unique call to women. Her desire is for God's healing and restoration to reach into women's lives in order that they may embrace all God desires to do through them. She is the author of the best-selling book *Fashioned for Intimacy*.

WANDA HANSEN, Washington, is the daughter-in-law of Jane Hansen.

HANNELORE ILLGEN, Germany, is on the Aglow International Board of Directors.

JOANNE MECKSTROTH, Alaska, is on the Aglow International Board of Directors.

DIANE MODER, Pennsylvania, is on the Aglow International Board of Directors.

NANCY McGUIRK, Maryland, is a United States director of Aglow International.

MARILYN REY, South Carolina, is a United States director of Aglow International.

EVELYN STEELE, Pennsylvania, is a United States director of Aglow International.

CAROL TORRANCE, Texas, is a United States director of Aglow International.

JEAN VANDENBOS, Colorado, is a United States director of Aglow International.

SANDRA WEZOWICZ, Connecticut, is a United States director of Aglow International.

MYSTEL WILLIAMSON is Jane Hansen's mother.

DEENA WILSON, Washington, is the author of *A Mom's Legacy: Five Simple Ways to Say Yes to What Counts Forever* (Regal Books).

International Contributors

National Presidents

BISI ADELUYI, Nigeria, Aglow National President

WINIFRED ASCROFT, Great Britain, Aglow National President

DOROTHY DANSO, Ghana, Aglow National President

MALVINE EVENSON, France, Aglow National President

GLADYS HARSHBARGER, Guatemala, former Aglow National President, Central America

ZEE JONES, Canada, Aglow National President, Aglow International Board of Directors

EGGRINAH KALIYATI, Zimbabwe, Aglow National President

TOVE MOMMER, Denmark, Aglow National President

JOAN MORTON, Australia, Aglow National President, International Board of Directors

JYTTE NIELSEN, Switzerland, Aglow National President

MERINO NETTO, India, Aglow National President, Aglow International Board of Directors

ANITA NORDSTROM, Sweden, Aglow National President

JANNIE REVERDA, Netherlands, Aglow National President

JANET ROBERTSON, New Zealand, Aglow National President, Aglow International Board of Directors

JACKIE SIMMONS, Hong Kong, Aglow National President

ISOBEL SMITH, Ireland, Aglow National President

EDDA SWAN, Iceland, Aglow National President

KRISTINA TURNER, Finland, Aglow National President

SYLVIA WEERASINGHE, Sri Lanka, Aglow National President

National Committee Presidents

SHANTI ADHIKARI, Nepal, Aglow National Committee President

ELIZABETH DAKA, Zambia, Aglow National Committee President

LILLA GERE, Hungary, Aglow National Committee President

MONIQUE VANDEN BLOOCK, Belgium, Aglow National Committee President

National Director

ANNETTE COOMBS, Caribbean South, Aglow National Director

Regional Directors

CELIA ESPIRITU, Philippines, Vice President of Ministries, Philippines National Board

TOWERA MASIKU, South East Africa, Aglow National Director

MOYA MICHALAKIS, Oman

Index